Michelangelo

Michelangelo

ROLF SCHOTT

LONDON
THAMES AND HUDSON

TRANSLATED AND ADAPTED FROM THE GERMAN
BY CONSTANCE McNAB

© THAMES AND HUDSON LONDON 1963
FIRST PAPERBACK EDITION 1964
SECOND IMPRESSION 1965
THIRD IMPRESSION 1971
FOURTH REPRINT 1975
PRINTED IN WEST GERMANY

ISBN 0 500 18019 9 clothbound
ISBN 0 500 20012 2 paperbound

CONTENTS

MICHELANGELO

Much has been written about the life and work of Michelangelo; his work has inspired constant curiosity about the man himself and about the spiritual problems and convictions expressed in his painting and sculpture. But only a few authors have attempted any detailed analysis of Michelangelo's inner vision, which is often deeper and more penetrating than that of other great artists. It was formed less by contact with his fellow-artists than by Dante's *Divine Comedy*, the Holy Scriptures, and the doctrines of Plato; by the tradition, as yet unbroken, of the dying Middle Ages, and by what was then known of Graeco-Roman art and civilization. The pressure of everyday existence has dimmed, for our generation, the memory of mankind's divine origin. Michelangelo's work is a visual statement of what the world has lost—the sense of wonder aroused by the mystery of human existence and human form.

As an artist, Michelangelo is impersonal. His visual work tells us nothing about the man himself or his environment. Personal suffering experienced, and endured; health, friendships, family affairs, nature and the topical events of his time—these things are not directly reflected in his paintings and sculptures, or even in those of his drawings which survived his death. They are revealed only in letters and poems, and even there, apart from an occasional very human outburst, they are referred to only in a reserved and stylized manner. In his art, they are so sublimated that it is not possible to discern the origins and inspirations of individual works.

This impersonal manner of self-expression was usual in Michelangelo's time, but it rarely took so unequivocal and emphatic a form. In the work of Verrocchio and Signorelli, even in Leonardo and Raphael, in Botticelli and Piero della Francesca, to say nothing of lesser masters, the outer world asserts itself far more, particularly in their sketches and drawings. Not so with Michelangelo. In his drawings especially, the model is merely used as a means of expressing an idea; it is stripped of all that is superfluous, acquired or merely incidental. This single-mindedness, which might strike some as being monotonous, enabled Michelangelo to outstrip his generation; it freed him from many of the limitations of his age. A man of essentially Gothic temperament, he gave to the supernatural a visual form which remained valid throughout the western world. Michelangelo has been called the father of Baroque, and even of Mannerism. Certainly all Baroque artists imitated him outwardly, but they seldom understood him.

Few contemporary biographers, even Condivi or Vasari, with both of whom he was friendly, give many details of Michelangelo's life. It is probably correct to assume that external happenings meant little to him; feeling, thought, achievement and meditation were more real to him than most of the actual events of his life, some of which were unhappy and confirmed him in his tendency to aloofness. The need which he often felt for escape from external situations caused him to leave many works half-finished. And even his work he rarely discussed with others.

Michelangelo, Michelagnolo or Michelangniolo to the Florentines, was born on 6th March 1475 at the castle of Caprese in the Tuscan province of Casentino. His father Ludovico di Leonardo Buonarroto Simoni, a rough and officious man and member of an old Tuscan

SAINT PROCULUS. 1494-5
SAN DOMENICO, BOLOGNA

SAINT PETRONIUS. 1494-5
SAN DOMENICO, BOLOGNA

family, held the office of Mayor of Chiusi and Caprese. The small boy was reared by a nurse at Settignano. His mother, Francesca di Neri di San Miniato del Sera, died very young, when the child was only six years old. After her death he was brought up without affection and frequently beaten. On showing signs of precocious gifts, Michelangelo was sent to school in Florence. Yielding with some misgivings to the boy's passion for drawing, his father entered him at the workshop of Domenico Ghirlandaio—Grillandaio in the Tuscan dialect—a well established, careful and somewhat prosaic painter of Florentine life and an able craftsman whose illustrative frescoes, especially those in the Gothic-Renaissance church of Santa Maria Novella which Michelangelo later liked to call his 'beloved bride', are well known to every lover of Italian art. Vasari called Ghirlandaio no less than 'the delight of his epoch'.

The harshness of his father and the early loss of his mother intensified Michelangelo's innate shyness and reserve and encouraged the habit of dealing silently with his inner struggles. An unassuaged longing for a mother's tenderness inclined him towards idealizing and exalting women. He was no doubt influenced by Dante's cult of Beatrice and Petrarch's adoration for Laura. Madonna figures, Sibyls, the famous 'Night', and his last, deeply moving symbolic groups of the 'Deposition', where the dead son sinks back into the arms of a mother spent in grief—all these testify to a chaste and sublimated love for women in whom he constantly saw the mother, and never, perhaps, the mistress or the beloved. This is borne out, too, by the undemanding friendship of the ageing Michelangelo for Vittoria Colonna, Marchesa of Pescara. In fact his only bride remained the Gothic shrine of the Virgin, and his own epithet is profoundly revealing. One extreme of his being is thus seen to have its origin in a solitary, withdrawn and devout contemplation. The other is to be looked for in his ancestral pride. He, who never founded a family, idealized the past history of his clan. His noble birth meant as much to him as his artistic genius, perhaps more. He believed passionately in a family tie with the Counts of Canossa and regarded as his illustrious forbears Beatrix, the sister of the Emperor Henry II, and the great Mathilda of Tuscany, in whose courtyard the barefooted Emperor Henry IV had begged absolution of Pope Gregory VII. Doubt has been cast upon the noble origin of the Buonarroti-Simoni but both Condivi and Vasari confirm it. Be that as it may, one might see in this conviction the second greatest motive force of his life. This patrician pride strengthened the father-fantasies which found expression in his frescoes of God the Father, in the 'Moses', Noah, the Prophets, the wrathful saints of the 'Last Judgement', and in Peter and Paul of his late frescoes. It was his way of idealizing his relationship with his brothers and his father, who were by no means endearing individuals and caused him much vexation and worry. These figures among others testify to his marked tendency to isolate himself from his surroundings and withdraw into an inner world; a world of faith, which was individual and his own. Michelangelo's pride in his nobility which masked an inner certainty of divine sonship, his unquenchable thirst for love and beauty, his melancholy and impressionable nature made him highly vulnerable, and therefore shy and withdrawn in self-defence.

Even while with Ghirlandaio, Michelangelo felt an inner compulsion to express himself more forcefully than was possible in the two-dimensional medium of painting; it spurred him on to master the third dimension by attempting sculpture. This step, taken in 1489, brought the gifted youth into closer contact with the cultured circle gathered at the court of the uncrowned king of Florence, Lorenzo il Magnifico. In the Medici Gardens near San Marco, adorned with antiques, he imbibed the intellectual climate of Neoplatonism evoked by the great artists and humanists whom in spite of his youth he was privileged to meet. There too, bitter misfortune assailed him in the person of the sculptor Torrigiani. This truculent bully, who later boasted of his brutal deed to Benvenuto Cellini, started an argument with Michelangelo, struck him across the face and smashed his nose. Whatever may have been the psychological effect of such a disfigurement, which remained with him for life, upon one who in his heart of hearts worshipped beauty, there can be little doubt that it accentuated the aloofness and independence of a character that was by nature reserved and introspective.

GHIRLANDAIO. BAPTISM OF CHRIST. DETAIL
SANTA MARIA NOVELLA, FLORENCE

It is not easy for us today to imagine a boy of fourteen or fifteen conversing with men like Angelo Poliziano, Cristoforo Landino, Marsilio Ficino or Pico della Mirandola. They may have sensed the fire that consumed him; at all events the effect on his work of such contacts testifies to the decisive influence exercised by these remarkable men; thinkers and poets who had been inspired and deeply affected not only by Plato, the sublime, but by the stormy sermons of a prophetic Dominican monk, Girolamo Savonarola.

GHIRLANDAIO. PRESENTATION IN THE TEMPLE. DETAIL
SANTA MARIA NOVELLA, FLORENCE

Such influences carried far more weight than those under which he
came in the workshops; to Ghirlandaio and Bertoldo di Giovanni of
the school of Donatello, Michelangelo owed more technical knowledge than art.   As an artist he was essentially self-taught, resembling
in this the Impressionists who, three hundred years later, learnt their
craft by studying and copying in the Louvre. Michelangelo studied
classical sculpture in the Medici Gardens, and perhaps the works of
Donatello and the makers of the doors for the Baptistery in Florence,

LEDA AND THE SWAN
MUSEO CIVICO CORRER, VENICE

mainly Lorenzo Ghiberti whose golden portals he called the gateway
to paradise. He loved his home town and its treasures, even when
the tyranny of later Medici rulers kept him away from it. Among
all the splendours of Rome and all the fame it brought him, he still
hankered after Florence.

MICHELANGELO'S EARLY WORKS AND HIS SURROUNDINGS

Allegedly Lorenzo de' Medici, il Magnifico or Sua Magnificenza, favoured the Buonarroti, father and son. He was well pleased with a
faun's mask by the young sculptor   (Not, as has been supposed, the

one displayed in the Bargello, which is not now considered an original work.) At all events, until the death of the ugly but irresistible and beauty-loving Medici the successful young artist was a member of his household and as such had access to all the splendours of Florentine life. But the disasters predicted by Savonarola were already casting their blight over the city and in due course the Medici with their followers were swept away, to make room for the repulsive French king Charles VIII and his court. Leafing through the diary of the pharmacist Luca Landucci, who kept a painstaking record of every event in Florence, great or small, we come to realize that in many ways the Renaissance was anything but a golden age. Florentine history is an unending chain of cruelty and folly, apparently aimed at the self-destruction of the entire noble caste. Vice, envy, spite and hatred were rife in a city seething with the passions, not only of its men of genius, but also of its numerous criminal elements, engrossed in a perpetual orgy of wild ambition, bloodshed, anger, pride and avarice, and in a continuous pageant of lavish displays and festivities. For several centuries, life here was more reckless and cruel than in ancient Rome or Athens, not to mention the many other, especially Italian, principalities of the Middle Ages. It is a miracle that this city, where justice was invariably sacrificed to political interest, did not suffer the fate it inflicted on so many others—conquest and destruction.

In 1478 the conspiracy of the Pazzi, secretly fostered by Pope Sixtus IV della Rovere, killed Lorenzo's popular and charming brother Giuliano and very nearly wiped out the entire Medici family. It was fearfully avenged. Blood flowed in the streets of Florence and tinted the waters of the Arno. At that time Michelangelo was still a child, and he grew up in troubled times. During his years of study in the Medici Gardens the city resounded with the exhortations and the eloquence of Savonarola. These grew more urgent after the death of Lorenzo il Magnifico. He had summoned Savonarola to his deathbed, but whether the preacher appeared there to judge or to bring consolation is not clear from the contradictory reports of the period.

In that same spring of the year 1492 Michelangelo returned to his father's house, but Lorenzo's son, Piero de' Medici, summoned him once more to his table, and during the cold winter of that year kept him occupied fashioning figures out of snow. One of Michelangelo's friends, a young man called Cardiere who sang pleasingly to the lute and was haunted by visions, twice saw the ghost of Lorenzo in a torn black habit. It ordered Cardiere to go to Piero de' Medici and tell him that he would soon be driven from his home, never to return. This eerie apparition was enough to rouse Michelangelo's supernatural fears and drive him from the tottering Medici court to Bologna, where he found a protector in the person of his compatriot Aldrovandi.

What Michelangelo thought of the world around him before his departure we do not know. Although they were not commissioned and he completed them of his own volition, the first works that have come down to us vaguely reflected his feelings and preoccupations. They are no more than exercises in various techniques, faintly reminiscent of the antiques in the Medici Gardens. Several works, among them a wooden 'Crucifixion', a marble 'Hercules' from Fontainebleau, an etching by Israel Silvester of 1677, and a copy of a 'Saint Anthony' by Schongauer, are lost. One pagan and one Christian relief have survived and already hint at the duality of his being. They are a 'Battle of the Centaurs', a high-relief worked in the round and overcrowded with too many figures, and the 'Madonna of the Stairs' in delicate low-relief; the former in the style of the school of Pisa and late Roman sarcophagi, the latter reminiscent of Hellenistic votive plaques, of Donatello's late reliefs and the delicate works of Florentine artists at the end of the Quattrocento.

One does not, however, get anywhere near understanding Michelangelo by quoting the sources of his inspiration. Naturally, in his early years he was not immune to influences exercised by his precursors and contemporaries, but even his initial attempts reveal an astonishing perfection and individuality. The 'Madonna of the Stairs' surprises us by the originality of its conception and the unusual composition. Not unlike an Etruscan mother-goddess (frequently depicted holding a child), the mother gazes fixedly into space, like some atavistic projection from the artist's unconscious. Is she

HEAD OF A FAUN. *c.* 1485
MUSEO NAZIONALE, FLORENCE

detached from life? Or secretly appalled by her Sibylline vision of the fate in store for the babe curled up and dozing in her lap? The mother seems to shield it with her garment, and, as Wölfflin points out, the child's head and arm rest at exactly the same angle as that of the dead Christ of the 'Pietà' in the Duomo of Florence. Why was the bridge introduced, with its playing children? Does it symbolize a transition? Does Michelangelo hint at a transformation of 'Maria Lactans' into the 'Madonna of the Pietà'? Does he wish to portray her austere and humble surrender? The term 'pietà' has a double significance—devout acceptance of divine decree and, in the arts, the portrayal of Christ in the lap of the Virgin after the deposition. In the vision of Christ's future martyrdom the child embodies a divine offering; indeed, the entire composition is an anticipation of the 'Pietà', and as such is unique in the history of western art. Its dignity is enhanced by the size of the female figure, contrasting with that of the children in the background. It seems pointless to dwell on minor defects, as for instance the hesitant treatment of the draperies or the right foot of the Virgin, which prove that technical mastery had not yet been attained. For it is clear that the youthful Michelangelo had already foreseen his ultimate direction, and that in the Pietà groups he was to return to his starting-point, the humble, yearning mother-and-son relationship. Are we then to understand that all we admire in his work is nothing but a digression? He indicates as much in some of his verses. It was an essential digression whereby the perishable was transformed through the work of art, itself a perishable thing, into the most sublime symbol of the Imperishable.

The other early work, and one which Michelangelo still valued in his old age, was a crowded relief of a combat between centaurs and lapiths or a similar theme, said to have been inspired by a poem by Poliziano. It shows a growing mastery in the treatment of an intricate group of male nudes. The undecided state of the battle is well conveyed and it is perhaps appropriate that the relief should never have been completed. Its most striking feature is the recurrence in a seemingly endless mass of moving bodies of certain attitudes which the artist developed in his later works. With the Mannerists they degenerated into pose and affectation, but they are almost exclusively the discovery of Michelangelo's genius, progressively evolved by him, although the composition of his youth was not repeated.

Michelangelo's next move was a journey to Bologna, presumably

MADONNA OF THE STAIRS. c. 1491
CASA BUONARROTI, FLORENCE

with a brief detour to Venice. It produced three memorable sculptures: two statues of saints and one angel bearing a candlestick, all three for the Arca di San Domenico. It was at this time too that Michelangelo discovered the portals of San Petronio by the Sienese Jacopo della Quercia.

These Bolognese sculptures of the young Michelangelo show a new pastose treatment of stone, especially noticeable in the drapery folds of the angel with the candlestick. The rich draperies of Saint Petronius and Saint Proculus, prefigured in the other statues of the shrine of San Domenico, probably imposed an irksome constraint on Michelangelo who was passionately interested in the anatomical study of dead bodies and the structure of the human form. Of the magnificent and fantastic draperies of later years there is as yet hardly any indication. Furthermore, his Bolognese period brought contact with Niccolò dell'Arca and his associates, who by then had already produced their major works. But the most important impetus came from the Sienese master Jacopo della Quercia who, like himself, had served his apprenticeship in Florence. Michelangelo never imitated others; he merely assimilated what he saw and recreated it in his own manner. Contact with Jacopo released new energy, although the Gothic flights of the older man, who died in 1483, did not directly affect Michelangelo's work. All the same, his influence was a lasting one and its impact made itself felt much later. A cherished memory of the exuberance of delicate yet powerful reliefs by della Quercia on the portal of Saint Petronius lingered in Michelangelo's mind, to be revived in the ceiling of the Sistine Chapel. During his first stay in the easy-going, hedonistic city of Bologna with its spreading arcades, the young artist was not sufficiently mature to emulate the great Sienese. Thus the sculptures carried out there under the protection of Aldrovandi are no more than modest exercises for his first great Roman and Florentine works. One thing in particular he learnt from della Quercia: how to bring gentleness and ease to the treatment of strong, massive and even crude figures in violent action. He did not altogether succeed with the 'Angel with Candlestick', which is bold and sturdy, with dough-like wings and draperies. It lacks the volatile charm of Tuscan angels

ANGEL WITH CANDLESTICK. 1494-5
SAN DOMENICO, BOLOGNA

of this type, though its general effect is clear and vigorous and it is
perfectly composed into an imaginary square. If it appears exceptionally robust it is because Michelangelo saw the heavenly host as
beings charged with vital energy rather than as airy spirits. His
'Saint Petronius' is an able and pleasing piece of sculpture which
would do credit to any artist; it is much too conventional for Michel-

BATTLE OF CENTAURS AND LAPITHS. *c.* 1491
CASA BUONARROTI, FLORENCE

angelo, though intimations of his future greatness are there. As for the grim, long-legged 'Saint Proculus', he already foreshadows Michelangelo's 'David'. Evidently Bologna with its tame brick palaces and red plaster was no place for the giant. Even his second stay there, which we shall discuss later, did not fall under a lucky star.

After the expulsion of the Medici the Florentine Republic was stabilized for a short time, and dedicated to Christ the King under the spiritual rule of the Prior of San Marco, the impressive Dominican preacher Girolamo Savonarola of Ferrara. It was a period contrasting with the usual run of events, full of sincere if gloomy enthusiasm, and fearful of the wrath of God. Although less hypocritical, it smacked of the later Calvinist régime in Geneva. The so-called *'piagnoni'*, weeping and howling penitents who predicted the Last Judgement and the Second Coming, set the general tone, and not a few secret enemies, especially the Franciscans, the classical opponents of the Dominican order (nicknamed the 'hounds of God'), observed these goings-on with scorn and derision. It was a régime definitely hostile to the arts and, as such, un-Florentine and anti-Roman; a régime that was bound to nettle the Spanish Pope Rodrigo Borgia, Alexander VI, a notorious personality but by no means adverse to the arts. The sharp attacks directed by Fra Girolamo against the amoral conduct of the Roman Pontiff and the Papal court were noted with displeasure, although for the time being ignored.

Michelangelo returned from Bologna to a Republic cleansed of all vestiges of the Medici rule and of the artistic treasures of the past by these same *'piagnoni'*—their ranks included men like Botticelli who, brought back to Christianity by Savonarola's preaching, returned to religious painting, and Lorenzo di Credi. He saw their pyres inexorably fed with works of art, books, and handsome bibelots. He fell prey to conflicting emotions: on the one hand a great urge to create beauty strengthened in Bologna by extensive reading of Dante, Petrarch and Boccaccio; on the other, a strong sympathy for the sincerity and zeal of the monkish régime. One of Michelangelo's brothers yielded so much to Savonarola's powers of persuasion that he joined the order. But Florence, where the young sculptor worked mainly on pagan compositions, offered no scope for his activities (his output at this time was small and has, in fact, been lost), and he felt compelled to leave, this time for Rome, where he arrived on 25th June 1496.

Now begins what might be termed Michelangelo's awe-inspiring ascent from the world of men into the towering realms of God. It is true that many obstacles and many an impasse faced him on this climb, but he never lost sight of his goal. Under the impact of Rome he entered a domain which Dante had relegated to limbo, but one which subsequent centuries, inspired by Antiquity, no longer regarded as a melancholy substitute Eden peopled by noble pagan ghosts excluded from the Christian universe; a golden age, rather, glorified by the humanist heirs of the scholastics. Michelangelo paid scant heed to events at the Papal court and the luxurious life of the clergy in the new Rome created by the enthusiastic planner Nicholas V Parentucelli. All he cared for were the artistic wonders of the classical world, especially certain recently excavated statues from Anzio, among them a marvellous Apollo, which Julius II later transferred to the Belvedere he had built in the Vatican Gardens. These splendid pieces, contrasting with the mannered products of his Tuscan homeland, were bound to have an intense effect upon Michelangelo. They won him over to Rome and, as an artist if not as a man, made him a Roman then and there, regardless of future interludes in Florence and other cities. If he says little on the subject, it does not indicate indifference. As usual, he remained silent, but his change of style speaks for itself.

But now something happened which is very characteristic of Michelangelo. The inspiration he derived from Antiquity far out-weighed the influences of, say, Giotto, Masaccio and Donatello. From its *disiecta membra* he produces his own completely original conception of the ancient world. His first sculpture in the classical style, a larger-than-life drunken Bacchus leaning on a small faun, probably a commission by the banker Jacopo Galli and intended for his garden, might at first sight seem an antique. And yet the fusion of naturalistic treatment and Praxitelean suavity do not result in a god, a brother of Apollo; not even a demi-god from the realm of Pan or Dionysus, but an elemental creature, weird and foolish, which might have come straight out of Tannhäuser's Venusberg. This sculpture may well be the fruit of a determination not to succumb to Savona-rola's magic but to remain faithful to the teachings of Ficino who regarded art as an act of worship and physical beauty as a reflection of the divine. Michelangelo's hurried departure from Florence was probably a flight from an atmosphere with which he felt a deep natu-ral affinity but which he meant to deny himself for the time being in order to extend his field of vision and experience. But his evo-cation of paganism in the 'Bacchus' remained a phantasmagoria.

While Michelangelo worked on the 'Bacchus' his inward eye must have been on classical statues, especially on the Apollo of the Belvedere, and it soon became clear that his technique was equal to that of the Greeks. At the same time he visibly seeks to deny the classical spirit, its radiant certainty and the ancient ideal of beauty. (Later he was to change, especially after his return to Rome, when he first saw the 'Laocoön', excavated in 1506.) The 'Bacchus' mystifies by a complete reversal of the artistic canon that informs the Apollo, and by a singular ambiguity achieved by unequivocal means. Although the disposition of one supporting leg and the other that takes no weight is that of a Greek statue, it fulfils no artistic function; the same is true of the shoulders, and the strong arms are limp and flaccid. On top of this there are the aggressive nakedness and bloated aspect of the handsome body, the glassy stare and foolish good looks, and the oblique avoidance of a frontal view. Indeed, the figure is best viewed in profile, with the faun in the foreground. It is that of a drunken youth without a shred of the nobility of the ancient gods; one whose lack of self-control is a little shaming. Can it have been a defiant gesture aimed at polytheism? No Greek or Roman sculptor would have envisaged a god in such terms; to do so would have been a sacrilege. And even though the Renaissance took passionately to reviving the old gods of Greece and Latium, they forthwith became fair game for a society reared on Christian aesthetics. Note how every detail of the 'Bacchus' is treated with masterly observation; how endearing the small faun, how luscious the ripe grapes cascading from the locks of the apparition. And yet the whole statue expresses an odd cheerlessness and vulnerability. It lacks precisely that quality which matured in Michelangelo during the completion of this great technical experiment: the quiet fervour of flesh and bone transfigured by the spirit and the miraculous handling of draperies of his first great 'Pietà'. The earlier work served to perfect his mastery of form, greater than that which went into the making of the Belvedere Apollo, which was an Augustan copy of some late Greek original. It is therefore unconvincing to date Michelangelo's 'Bacchus' after his 'Pietà', as some scholars have done.

BACCHUS. DETAIL. 1496-7
BARGELLO, FLORENCE

PIETA. 1501
SAINT PETER'S, ROME

On a drawing by Marten van Heemskerk the 'Bacchus' is still seen standing in the cortile of the Casa Galli; the right hand is missing, perhaps intentionally so as to pass it off as an antique.

During that period Michelangelo had two other distinguished patrons: the Cardinals Riario and Jean de Bilhères de Lagraulas, the French ambassador to the Holy See. This devout nobleman commissioned the 'Pietà' for the French chapel in Saint Peter's. His expectations were high and were amply fulfilled. Placed not too well and rather high inside the first right-hand chapel of Saint Peter's, it made Michelangelo overnight the most celebrated sculptor of Christendom. It was his first unequivocal statement of artistic and religious beliefs. That the artistic and religious elements formed an indivisible whole is self-evident. The group is a symbol, and the quintessence of the Christian faith; it might be described as the nearest thing to a monstrance rendered in terms of human life.

The master had chosen a theme found less often in 15th-century Italy than in the Gothic North. He re-created and raised it to heights of naturalistic and spiritual perfection not since surpassed—unless it be by himself, although in an entirely different and marvellously muted key. Such harmony and skill in the representation of divine presence had perhaps never been attained, unless in early Greek or Chinese art. We find it here in a young artist who, at the age of twenty-six, undertook to wrest the most sublime meaning from a block of Carrara marble. He signed his work, perhaps only this once, by cutting his name into the shoulder band of the Madonna with the proud and caressing gesture of a son drawn close to his mother.

Clad in the wide mantle dear to Gothic tradition, the Holy Virgin rests on a rock and holds the dead body of the Lord, her son, encircling and sustaining him with her right arm, while the gesture of her left arm with its opening hand expresses everything: sadness and self-surrender, consent and mystery, a wordless communication addressed to the whole of mankind. The delicacy and balance of the group defies description; every fold, every gesture contains an entire world and the whole effect is of such perfection that it was matched once only, in the 'Madonna and Child' of Notre Dame at Bruges.

Michelangelo finished both groups—a thing he rarely did—without imparting too much smoothness to this superbly beautiful Madonna. He must have had the jeweller's touch—inherited from the early Etruscans; but also the searching hands of the healer and the lover, the fingers of a perfect instrumentalist.

Two objections have been raised against the 'Pietà': why all those draperies and why so young a mother for a son thirty-three years old? To the first we reply that the helpless nakedness of Jesus is thrown into relief and made more precious by being laid in the shrine of her robe. The other was answered by Michelangelo himself, in reply to a question by Ascanio Condivi. A chaste and undefiled being would not age; such are not subject to the laws of time and matter. Perhaps there was some theological speculation in Michelangelo's words, the more so as he added that the son, because it had been thus decreed, was subject to these very laws. These are valid reasons, but what Michelangelo quite clearly struggled to express was his own unfulfilled longing, that longing for his mother which, as it were, could not be assuaged save perhaps in death. When his mother died she was the age of the Madonna of the 'Pietà', while the son—that is, the young artist—is portrayed as the Mediator and Redeemer returned by death into the mother's arms. Such feelings are anything but blasphemous, for all true insight must derive from individual experience. One thing is certain: the noble group is overflowing with infinite tenderness. Not a square inch of it but is instinct with meaning; every trace of light and shadow radiates a spiritual quality.

There were several peak periods in Michelangelo's art, and therefore also in his life. In a man of genius the two could hardly be separated. His contemporaries had begun to notice him, but even then he could not settle down in Rome. Flattering commissions may have been offered from Florence. He no longer felt in danger there, as the Republic had quietened down at last after fearful upheavals. The abortive 'rule of God' had come to an end with the

PIETA. DETAIL

burning of its advocate at the stake. The worthy and rather pedestrian Piero Soderini became Gonfaloniere of the Signoria. Possibly Michelangelo harboured a secret desire to study the works of his rival, the mysterious and ubiquitous Leonardo da Vinci, a man as lonely as himself but his elder, and his superior in experience and knowledge of the world. Perhaps he longed to measure his strength against that of Leonardo. They were certainly not made to understand each other. Michelangelo was not exactly easy to get on with. Yet he gained something from Leonardo, especially when the Republic set the two geniuses in competition, commissioning each to paint a battle scene on opposite walls of the Great Council. Although Michelangelo disliked painting, he was anxious to defeat his most powerful rival. And in fact destiny decreed that he should become a unique master of this art.

After an absence of five years, Michelangelo arrived in Florence on 19th July 1501. He then set about fulfilling a commission for the cathedral of Siena from Cardinal Francesco Piccolomini, the future Pope Pius III: a series of minor statues, able works but nothing more, only four of which Bastio da Montelupo carried out from his designs. Static figures of saints were not his forte. It is thought that the 'Madonna and Child' of Bruges was also planned for the Piccolomini altar. As the commission for it, whether from Flanders or Florence, had been given in Rome, it is probable that he began it there before his departure. Although the 'Madonna of Bruges' is less than life-size, and in spite of a slightly altered technique, her mood is related to that of the Roman 'Pietà'. Which is the more sublime it is difficult to say, but Bruges may deem itself fortunate indeed in having had the merchant magnate Mouscron secure this treasure in 1506. Various influences, ranging from Donatello and della Quercia to the Flemish painters, have been seen in this work. Yet this Virgin with the wonderful Child differs from all former sculptures of its kind. In painting, too, nothing comparable exists, unless it be Leonardo's 'Madonna of the Rocks', which Michelangelo probably never saw since it had long been kept in Milan. What he absorbed from other artists was never their manner of composition or technique, but their strength and greatness, which he then surpassed. He thought as

MADONNA AND CHILD. *c.* 1504
NOTRE DAME, BRUGES

Leonardo did: 'Lamentable the pupil who does not outshine his master.'

The more compact Madonna of Bruges reverses the situation depicted in the Roman 'Pietà'. The Christ Child stands on his own feet and is full of life, while the mother is remote, mysterious, as though belonging to a different realm, like the dead carved on Attic funeral stelae. She gazes past the child; her gaze is turned inward, detached and wise, beyond all earthly feelings. The child, about to venture out into the world, reaches almost playfully with its left hand for reassurance from the mother, who knows that the book she guards in her right hand contains the secret of the lives of mother and son and of all humankind. Here too the child, which resembles her, is wrapped in the rich folds of her robe, more clearly modelled than those of the 'Pietà'. Upon the Madonna's head Michelangelo has focused every tender memory of his mother, disposing the hair—slightly damaged at the nape of the neck—the veil and kerchief round the enchanting countenance of a somewhat grave young girl. Again we can read into the work something of the artist's life; of the moment when the small boy was forced into a loveless existence, while the young mother vanished into the realm of shades.

In this piece of sculpture Michelangelo's early style found its full expression, and it shows that he had already gone a long way. It was now seven years since his teacher, Domenico Ghirlandaio, had been buried in the church of Santa Maria Novella which he had adorned so handsomely. With his next work, Michelangelo began to leave this phase behind and move in a new direction, motivated at first by a spirit of revolt and grim struggle. Before it became a battle with his rival it was a battle with a block of marble spoilt by one of Agostino di Duccio's pupils which the Signoria had commissioned him to use for a statue of David. He set to work and had soon produced a figure bold and defiant to the point of gruesomeness. The youthful David with the sling became a naked—and presumably victorious—Goliath, or one of those mythical heroes fathered by a god on a mortal. The Florentines at once had a name for the

MADONNA AND CHILD. DETAIL

35

DAVID. 1501-4
ACCADEMIA, FLORENCE

DAVID. DETA

RUBENS. BATTLE OF ANGHIARI, AFTER LEONARDO DA VINCI

athlete, alert and poised, with the arms of a wrestler and the eagle eye of the all-seeing Apollo; it was *'il gigante'*.

On Michelangelo's contemporaries this statue had the effect of a thunderbolt. It roused much opposition and was even stoned; for some considerable time it had to be guarded. Like all Michelangelo's works it contains an element of the divine, but more deeply hidden than in any other. In token of the Commune's desire to protect its citizens, as David had protected his people, a commission had chosen for the giant a site right in front of the equally bold Palazzo Vecchio instead of the pilaster of the Duomo originally intended for it. Not a bad political allusion. But what the artist meant to say springs to the eye: 'This is I, and thus we are! Be on your guard!' Landucci says that the statue was 'ready and fully unveiled' on 8th September 1504. During the street fighting of 1526 on the Piazza, the giant's right arm was damaged. Today a copy has taken the place of the original, removed to the Academy in 1878 for protection from the weather. This statue makes it clear for the first time why the Italians called their greatest sculptor '*il terribile*'; why he inspired such awe and fear. Though it has affinities with classical sculpture the angular, rebellious, disturbingly naked figure is not beautiful. The backward bend, more apparent than real, makes it appear slightly lopsided and the straddling leg is almost repellent. The superbly fashioned hands are those of a killer. But in spite of its naturalism, the general effect is overpowering because of a stupendous tension and élan.

A. DA SANGALLO. BATTLE OF CASCINA, AFTER A CARTOON BY MICHELANGELO
HOLKHAM HALL, THE EARL OF LEICESTER

SAINT MATTHEW. *c.* 1505
ACCADEMIA, FLORENCE

In contrast to the 'David' statues of Donatello and Verrocchio, Michelangelo represents the youth not after but before his victory, thereby creating one of the most dramatic figures of all time.

Here we can see that the artist composed not by piecing together but by eliminating, in order to arrive at the quintessence of a figure. For Michelangelo, more than for any of his predecessors, the human body was a thing formed and animated by a play of forces; a thing of balanced contrasts, to be expressed contrapuntally. As he did not proceed by piecing together, he worked practically always directly from the marble block. His perfect knowledge of internal structure and anatomy was unsurpassed in his day. At the same time he rose above the autonomy of nature, ascending towards the post-classical daemonic concept of the divine. Hence his work expresses, not enthusiasm but Titanic rebellion and the pathos of loneliness; not humour but bitterness and renunciation. And yet it radiates a nameless beauty; the pristine beauty of man in the Garden of Eden, perhaps never expressed so perfectly in the history of art.

He did not carry out the monumental order of 1503 from the Weavers' Guild for twelve large statues of Apostles for the chapels of the Duomo. As we have said, he was not cut out for creating static figures wrapped in pious meditation. This is confirmed by the famous 'Saint Matthew', the only one of these statues carried out, and even that left unfinished. This almost uncanny fragment, arrested as if by some evil magic, gives an impression of dynamic stillness, of an incredible display of movement made to express recollection, and possibly pain and sorrow. In spite of the Book of Holy Scripture emerging from the stone, the beholder cannot help asking himself whether this figure really represents an Evangelist. If, as some scholars believe, it was begun in Rome about 1506 or in Florence soon after under the impact of the newly excavated 'Laocoön' and the 'Menelaus-Pasquino', it would mean that here Michelangelo indulged for the first time in outright imitation of the antique. This would be out of keeping with his character, all the more so since the likeness between the statues is a superficial one. The restlessness and searching of his Florentine period may have found expression in the treatment of Saint Matthew. Michelangelo was overwhelmed with work and felt compelled to try his hand at violent contrasts, at gentle and turbulent, sacred and profane, spiritual and political themes. In brief, the 'Saint Matthew' who never fully emerged from the rock fits well into the period of the 'Bathing Soldiers', which we shall now discuss.

Michelangelo's 'David' had turned out to be a civic symbol. The invitation to compete with Leonardo in the Council Chamber of the Palazzo Vecchio had a background of historico-political propaganda. The chosen theme was a victorious battle of Florentine forces, to wit, that of Cascina, while Leonardo, who had been summoned earlier, was working on a 'Battle of Anghiari. Strangely enough the cool and composed Leonardo, a man superior to even the best among his contemporaries, produced a faultless composition of a furious mounted battle raging round a standard (an etching by Edelingk of a splendid copy in chalk by Rubens shows the astounding compactness of the design), while the combative and aggressive Michelangelo restrained himself and chose to portray soldiers bathing in the Arno, surprised and hurriedly dressing to meet an attack of the Pisans.

Evidently the Gonfaloniere Soderini had given the two artists a free hand with the details of their theme. By then Leonardo had completed his stupendous 'Last Supper' in Milan, not to speak of other compositions with many figures, whereas Michelangelo's only attempt at the treatment of interlocking masses of male bodies was the 'Battle of the Centaurs', which was an early work and not altogether successful. Now he was asked to cover a huge wall 17.5 metres wide and 7 metres high with figures in motion; he was made to use colour, though he had abandoned painting long ago. Ghirlandaio had composed frescoes with multiple figures and had shown his pupils how it was done, but his figures hardly ever bore more than a decorative relation to each other, and took little account of perspective. The new style made quite different demands. How was he, Michelangelo, to cover the distance that separated him from Leonardo without showing his lack of experience? Leonardo had been the first to solve the new problem of composition in perspective. Boldly, and without heeding Leonardo's chiaroscuro and his treatment of colour, Michelangelo set to work on the gigantic cartoon.

But both artists soon tired of their task, perhaps because they found it irksome and intolerable to work together in the same hall, and left before their work was finished, Leonardo for Milan and Michelangelo for Rome. It is scarcely surprising therefore that in spite of the enthusiasm of the Florentines these drawings have not been preserved. We have only old prints of Marco Antonio Schiavonetti and Agostino Veneziano and a copy kept at Holkham Hall to go by in assessing what Michelangelo achieved. It is mainly a matter of conjecture. Looking at the pastiche of the worthy and somewhat dry Schiavonetti which combines bits of Michelangelo's composition with the landscape of Dutch graphic art, one gains the impression that Michelangelo treated the theme as a sculptured relief, concentrating on sharp outlines and neglecting colour, space, light and perspective. It evidently became a series of interlacing nudes, a tightly compressed study of male anatomy; virtually an imposing and unconscious exercise for his future undertaking, carried through on a much higher spiritual level in the Sistine Chapel. There he presumably began with the fresco of the 'Deluge', which is most closely related to the 'Bathers' and comparatively the weakest of the ceiling frescoes.

Michelangelo's cartoon had more success with the artists of the time than did that of Leonardo. As a representation of animated, almost Mannerist nudes it was more modern than the work of Leonardo, his senior by twenty-three years, a man of almost superhuman stature and an enigma even to the élite of the day. His ultimate spiritual agony and suffering, his reaction against his own early development and, above all, against the gay, sophisticated pageant of the world around him still lay before Michelangelo, to be developed in the Medici tombs, and finally in the 'Last Judgement'. Meanwhile, he was still a young man and his cartoon of the 'Bathers' was acclaimed as 'la scuola del mondo' and the acme of anthropomorphic self-glorification. But he himself never borrowed from others and his study of living or dead models had nothing to do with the copying from nudes that was then already customary. He did not copy figures and postures from nature or from classical models, but by sheer concentration, both meditative and intuitive (no doubt

THE PITTI MADONNA. c. 1505
BARGELLO, FLORENCE

accompanied by marginal notes and sketches), transformed what he saw into clear and definite concepts; a noble, classical store of visual images whose very wealth increasingly oppressed him. Historical subjects and the obliging Soderini as Maecenas did not suffice. What he needed was the stimulus of Christian and mythological themes, and a master of the calibre of Julius II.

Before passing on to his Roman period we must examine three minor works which were completed at this time, together with his greater Florentine achievements. They are two sculptured *tondi* which, as usual, remained unfinished, and a painted one. All are supposed to have been influenced by a secret study of Leonardo. That may well be, but Michelangelo did not try to enter Leonardo's mind; he did not share Raphael's naïve unconcern over learning and copying from others. The marble relief of the 'Madonna of Taddeo Taddei' is the most serene and lovely thing he ever made. As not a single stroke of Michelangelo's chisel lacked significance he must have been, to use Nietzsche's expression, 'superficial from his depths', using the motive of children playing with a bird in a symbolic sense. The *Bambino* seems frightened of the fluttering bird; it is as though John were making demands upon his spirit which he intuitively dreads. (The graceful mother with the turban may have inspired many an 'English style' picture.)

In the 'Madonna of Bartolommeo Pitti' the Virgin's head extends beyond the rim of a circular relief, thereby emphasizing her prophetic expression. The rim is resumed on the Virgin's forehead with a design of a winged seraph or cherub. The Madonna is of heaven and earth. She sits on a low, square block of stone. The expression on her face is stern (and perhaps not altogether a success artistically), and the child sadly buries his head in his hand. John the Baptist fades away in the background. The third of the three *tondi* is the strongest. The 'Madonna Doni' is a miracle of sculptural drawing and artistic skill, carried out in sharply defined primary colours, distinctly stated down to the last detail and at the same time rich in objective symbolism, and geometrical in design, even though as yet nowhere near to possessing the colourful splendour of the Sistine Chapel. The violently twisted, complicated figure of the Virgin on whose shoulder the

RAPHAEL. POPE JULIUS II
UFFIZI GALLERY, FLORENCE

child has been raised as future Victor and Ruler, indicates the worldly
and otherworldly nature, the timelessness of the Holy Family, in
which the noble head of Joseph stands for God the Father in the
Trinity. The seed of Mannerism is sown here—though its essential
meaning was misunderstood by those who were later to adopt the
style. Leonardo's triangular composition has become the base of a
pyramid. The background is given to the naked and unselfcon-
scious pagan world of Platonic Love, while on the right Saint John
looks adoringly at his raised companion from behind a low wall.

THE TADDEI MADONNA. *c.* 1504
ROYAL ACADEMY, LONDON

Occasionally—and fortunately—it happens that a Head of State is remembered for what he did as a private individual rather than for his achievements in war or politics. Everybody knows that Julius II was a great Renaissance Pope with military ambitions, but today the fame of this high priest of Christendom, better known in his own day as a soldier and warlord than a cleric, is almost exclusively a reflection of the achievements of the artists he employed—Buonarroti, Bramante and Raphael. It rests on the new church of Saint Peter and the Vatican buildings, the frescoes on the ceiling of the Sistine Chapel, his own mausoleum, and the frescoes in the *Stanze di Raffaello*.

Giuliano della Rovere, Cardinal of San Pietro in Vincoli, ascended the Papal throne in his sixtieth year. He was an irate, awe-inspiring, iron-willed giant; never small-minded, but tormented by gout and venereal disease like his predecessors Pius II Piccolomini and Alexander VI, the Borgia Pope who had fathered several children. Power and magnificence, especially the material possession of his spiritual domain, and of course his family, were what mattered to him. Advice of any sort he would generally shun. At the head of his own troops, he spared neither himself nor them in an all-out bid to drive the French from Italy, which he hoped to unite under his rule. The outcome was that the Spaniards, who were far worse enemies than the French, were able to enter by the back door.

At first the Pope's favourite architect was Antonio da Sangallo, an able man who knew Michelangelo from the Medici Gardens and both admired and supported him. This architect who, in the words of Jakob Burckhardt, 'accomplished remarkable things with moderate means,' recommended Michelangelo to the Pontiff. Michelangelo's design for a monumental mausoleum for the apse of the old church of Saint Peter was submitted, in spite of the fact that the aged Pope disliked being reminded of death.

In March 1505, we find Michelangelo back in Rome charged with proceeding immediately with his plans, and despatched to Carrara to secure the marble for the basic construction and the statues. His fee of 10,000 ducats was either never paid or spent on the material.

THE DONI TONDO
UFFIZI GALLERY, FLORENCE

Everything turned out differently from what he had expected. By the time he returned to Rome in 1506 and deposited his first consignment of marble in Saint Peter's Square the Lombard architect Bramante, a relative of Raphael's, had gained ascendency at the Vatican; Sangallo shortly afterwards retired to Florence. Unfortunately Michelangelo saw in Bramante a sort of evil genius intent on harming him in every way. Certainly, there was rivalry, but it was not, as he imagined, a life and death struggle. Julius II was determined to realize the project first put forward by his predecessor Nicholas V Parentucelli, and replace the venerable but sadly derelict early Christian Basilica of Saint Peter by a new church which would include his own mausoleum. Bramante drew the basic plans. Michelangelo saw in all this nothing but spite and envy. This was hardly just—neither, on the other hand, was the Pope's treatment of his protégé. Haughty and capricious, he failed to inform Michelangelo of his latest decisions and refused to see him. After the fifth attempt to gain a hearing, Michelangelo was asked by a Palace servant to leave the Vatican. Julius II was unreliable and egocentric, and these traits got the better of his undoubted esteem and affection for the artist. Small wonder that the choleric and melancholy Michelangelo was overcome by fury, disappointment and disgust. Conscious of his unique ability and genius, and perhaps even more of his noble birth, he rebelled against such treatment from a fellow-noble. As a true Florentine, he abhorred anything that smacked of tyranny. He sent the Pope a sharp reply and rode away. In Florence he felt safe enough from the ill-tempered Pope, who had meanwhile despatched an irate letter of complaint to the Signoria.

What Michelangelo did during the ensuing period is not quite clear. The cartoon in the Signoria had been completed and there seems to have been some delay over the painting. But such creative intervals were necessary to him from time to time, and there is every reason to believe that during this period of so-called inactivity his mind was furiously active. Some biographers have stated—surely incorrectly—that Michelangelo was poorly educated. If it were not enough that he conducted his correspondence in Latin and was known as an expert on Dante, his art surely proves that his knowledge

IGNUDO
SISTINE CHAPEL

increased constantly in scope and depth. His intellectual growth was a natural rather than a forced one; he showed wisdom and intuitive knowledge rather than the learning that distinguishes theologians and scholars.

In Florence he toyed with the idea of evading the Papal court once and for all by accepting an invitation from Sultan Bayazid II to build a bridge across the Golden Horn at Constantinople. But in November 1506, as though obeying an inner urge, he roused himself and literally met half-way the Pope's summons to return, proceeding, not actually to Rome, but to Bologna. Julius II arrived there at the beginning of the month, after having driven out the reigning family of Bentivoglio. In a letter written in 1524, after Julius' death, a disgruntled Michelangelo describes the trouble the Pope caused him, and accuses him of having been the cause of his economic worries and lost opportunities, asserting that he was forced to come to Bologna 'with a rope round his neck'. He goes on to complain of the work 'on the ceiling of San Sisto' and of outstanding or insufficient payments. It was another instance of his habit of making heavy weather of the very real difficulties of his existence. He knew but at the same time failed to appreciate the fact that the Pope's intuition spurred him on to unparalleled achievements. True, much remained unfinished and, although there were indeed obstacles, both men are partly to blame for this. When the Pope finally commissioned Michelangelo to adorn the Sistine ceiling with paintings, he was offering him a unique opportunity to express a host of ideas which it would have needed several lifetimes to express in the medium of stone. Michelangelo was seldom satisfied with anything; he seemed to be haunted by his idea of a truly noble, perfect society—perhaps a longing sown in his mind by Plato. If we bear this in mind, Michelangelo's weaknesses may be regarded as no more than the stains that gather upon the mantle of all who make the arduous journey back to the divine source of being.

The reconciliation between the Pope and his favourite artist took place in Bologna. There must have been a certain style and humour about their meeting; and the Pope comes out of it best. When Michelangelo attempted to justify his absence, Julius' face darkened.

Whereupon a cleric who was present tried to intervene by saying that Michelangelo ought to be excused since, as an artist, he was lacking in manners and *savoir-faire*. The Pontiff turned on his minion: how could he abuse the artist in a way which he himself would never have done? And showed him the door. Michelangelo was back in favour with a commission for a bronze statue, 4 metres high, of the new lord of Bologna. The 3,000 ducats he was paid for it were hard-earned. Misery and pestilence reigned in the city. The first cast was unsuccessful. On 21st February the new statue was set above the centre porch of San Petronio, and Michelangelo left at once for Florence and Rome. We have no more than a vague idea of what the statue was like. A Pope enthroned to bless and rule is hard to fit into Michelangelo's *œuvre*. Three years later the Bentivoglio were back in Bologna and on 30th December 1511 they had the figure taken down and destroyed. The fragments went into the foundries of Alfonso of Ferrara. Only the head was saved and stored in the duke's cabinet, but it has long since been lost.

A PAINTER IN SPITE OF HIMSELF: THE CEILING OF THE SISTINE CHAPEL

Between 1506 and 1508 Michelangelo returned frequently to the idea of a mausoleum for Julius II, and after his reconciliation with the Pope he no doubt hoped that something would come of these grandiose plans. Meanwhile the marble blocks disappeared one by one from Saint Peter's Square. When he returned to Rome the Pope would not hear of the project, the more so as the new church of Saint Peter was nowhere near completion, quite unready for the monumental tomb. The walls were probably not higher than the one Remus jumped in mockery of his brother Romulus.

Instead, the Pope peremptorily called upon Michelangelo to paint the ceiling of the Sistine Chapel, fixing for the work a fee of 15,000 ducats; a not inconsiderable sum for the parsimonious Julius. In vain did Michelangelo, suspecting a new wile of Bramante behind it all, protest that he was no painter; that this was not his form of art. Bramante, he felt, was hoping that he would either refuse and fall

HEAD OF THE PROPHET JOEL
SISTINE CHAPEL

into disgrace, or accept and become a laughing-stock—suspicions
that were probably unjustified. As it was, things turned out quite
differently. The sculptor summoned all the resources of his vast
talents, and showed himself to be a peerless painter: a painter addicted
to contour and tactile values, it is true, but with an unerring feeling
for concord between optical effect and the symbolic implications of
colour. He was seized by a compulsive urge; years of both torment
and joy, of wellnigh ceaseless activity began.

HEAD OF THE PROPHET EZEKIEL
SISTINE CHAPEL

Julius II was very fond of his private chapel. He had consecrated it himself and dedicated it to the Assumption of the Virgin on 15th August 1483, when his uncle, Sixtus IV, dreaded Simoniac and great patron of architects, still sat upon the Papal throne. The Sistine Chapel had no architectural distinction, being badly proportioned, and rather like a vaulted barn, with wall spaces broken up by unimportant cornices and pilasters. It had been decorated by a host of distinguished Florentine and Umbrian painters; Papal por-

CEILING OF THE SISTINE CHAPEL. 1508-12
SISTINE CHAPEL

[handwritten annotations: Judith / Zacharias / David and Goliath / Delphic Sibyll / Joel / Isaiah / Erythraean Sibyll / Cumaean Sib / Ezec... / ...]

traits adorned the upper part of the walls. In the centre were frescoes from the lives of Christ and of Moses, with below a *trompe-
l'œil* of gilt tapestries copied from Byzantine designs. The vault,
decorated with spandrels, was sky-blue, inset with golden stars;
the floor was inlaid with coloured mosaics. A magnificent marble
screen divided the presbytery from the nave, and there was an
attractive choir. These things had been there since the time when
Melozzo da Forlí portrayed, in a lovely fresco showing the founding
of the Vatican library, the youthful Giuliano, tall and handsome in
his purple cloak, his energetic mouth already showing the lines
which were to become so characteristic. Dominating the scene,

Daniel   Libyan Sibyll   Jonah

Persica   Jeremiah

he stands in front of the coldly imposing figure of Sixtus della Rovere (who very nearly secularized his office and the Papal state), while the humanist archivist Platina can be seen kneeling beside him.

It was an enchanting Quattrocento interior, both contemplative and spiritual; there was no doubt about that. The aged Pope, however, sensed the coming of the new age; he set his mind on something more impressive than a starred heaven fit for simple minds. But he had no definite plans in mind. Or had he? What about some Apostles? Michelangelo had had quite enough of Apostles in Florence. We know what happened to the Saint Matthew, the only one of the twelve to be carved—and left half-imprisoned within

57

Eve. Detail

the stone. 'That will be a poor effort, Your Holiness,' murmured Michelangelo. 'Why?' asked the Pope. 'Because Apostles are poor,' replied Michelangelo, jokingly for once. 'Do as you please,' growled the Pope and left. Michelangelo in fact did as he pleased— a quite unheard-of thing. He created, as he said himself, not with his hands but with his mind. It is unlikely that he allowed himself to be guided by the advice of others. He simply took the entire basic concept for Julius' mausoleum and flung it lock, stock and barrel upon the chapel ceiling, without consideration for himself and his health, for the peaceful character of the place, or the works of earlier and simpler masters (the altarpiece was still Perugino's 'Assumption of the Virgin'), without a thought for the people who would crane their necks and strain their eyes to see his Titanic creations. And is there sufficient compensation for all this and for much else which rouses our misgivings? Of course there is, provided we approach it with a mind that is receptive both to the aesthetic and the spiritual implications.

Goethe, for one, did precisely this. On 23rd August 1787 he noted down in Rome: 'Without having seen the Sistine Chapel one can form no appreciable idea of what *one* man is capable of achieving.'

While working out the composition of the ceiling Michelangelo must have been constantly spurred on by his visions, and even the process of planning and reflection happened with unwonted speed. Eventually he left behind all his acquired knowledge and theology, the theories of Dante and Neoplatonic doctrine. We are faced with a miracle. Everything centres round the human being; the rest is more sketchy than a Shakespearean scene. Michelangelo's inner vision compensated him for all the miseries of his personal life. Of course such a man could not remain blind to the horrors of existence. He knew what it was to be one of God's favoured children; but he also knew what it was to be temporarily disowned, a son fallen from grace, living in filth and degradation. This contrast tormented Michelangelo no less than it tormented the Prophets of his vision, and the beholder must inevitably sense this torment. The Sistine Chapel contains 343 figures. They took four years to complete; one figure every four days or so—and what a figure! It

NUDE STUDY FOR THE SISTINE CHAPEL CEILING
TEYLER MUSEUM, HAARLEM

CREATION OF WOMAN
SISTINE CHAPEL

must be remembered that Michelangelo's figures do not belong to the race of the weary and heavy-laden; they are messengers from another world—the world of the spirit. Consider, too, that the ceiling, carried out against his will, is the only large, completely finished composition of Michelangelo's that we have. The 'Last Judgement' he also completed, but it is a painting on a single theme. The Sistine ceiling is the picture of pictures, as the Bible is the book of books. Tolnay was right in calling it 'the Divine Comedy of the Renaissance'.

What is its subject, and what does it express and symbolize? Michelangelo took into account the construction of the Chapel, and, in the *trompe-l'œil* configuration of the ceiling, extended it into a transcendent sphere, mindful that it was dedicated to the Assumption of the Blessed Virgin. A row of pilasters ends in spandrels flanked by thrones: the thrones of seven Prophets and five Sibyls instead of the Apostles proposed by the Pope. These universal figures in the classical style are animated by the new Renaissance spirit, and each of them is an individual. They form the outer frame for the long rectangle of the vaulted ceiling, divided into four large and five smaller fields, nine in all.

Between the prophetic figures and along the walls are spandrels and lunettes whose frescoes form part of the central composition. This section belongs to the abandoned plans for the Papal mausoleum. The figures have been altered but without losing the basic idea: the concept of a world theatre, representing three levels of creation in man fashioned by God, namely his body, soul and spirit. The idea is an ancient one and goes back to pre-Christian, in particular Hellenic civilization.

In order to introduce order and clarity into the design with its wealth of movement, a *trompe-l'œil* architectural structure has been added. It is a gigantic oblong in white, framed by the pointed spandrels, crossed by ten beams spreading over the entire vault. The rest is achieved by the contrasting size of the fields and the differing use of colour in the various zones. The general effect is classical and biblical, timeless and transcendent.

In order to express all three levels of man's divine inheritance in terms of human forms, Michelangelo placed in the spandrels and lunettes a chronicle of mankind, personified by the ancestors of Jesus and illustrated in simple, homely scenes; and, in the four corner spandrels, tragic events from the history of Israel, which illustrate the bondage of man after the Fall, fettered by the material world. Above and closer to the centre extends the sphere of the souls; the illustrious assembly of Prophets and Sibyls who contemplate

HEAD OF THE PROPHET JONAH
SISTINE CHAPEL

the divine and have inspired knowledge of what is decreed for venia , unaware humanity: it is the zone of the awakened ones to whom applies the much abused Nietzschean epithet of 'superman'. The uppermost central zone that skirts the parting of the vault shows the sphere of divine self-begetting and creation, including God and man and the mystery of the Fall which led to the Deluge and Noah's degradation, but also to the Patriarch's offering as a portent of redemption and re-union with God. This transcendental zone is rendered remote by skilful use of perspective, while the awakened ones, the seers and prophetesses of the middle zone, are intensely present and alive. These tangible and still highly classical presences extend to the highest sphere, where twenty naked youths enact the beatitude of the heavenly world and fulfil a figurative rather than decorative function: they are ornaments in a serenely heroic style. Condivi calls them the *'ignudi'*. They have been wrongly described as slaves.

But it should be remembered that on the ceiling of the Sistine Chapel Michelangelo, who was a devout and practising Catholic, illustrated his faith, using mythology, philosophy and the Old Testament to create a vision that was utterly his own and therefore fresh. It was visually so overpowering and convincing that, quite apart from the data of Christian cosmogony and teaching, the Occident has come to visualize the spiritual world and its inhabitants in the form that Michelangelo gave them: the visual expression of an approach to life whose vitality has so far withstood all contrary philosophies and social doctrines. Even Leonardo and Raphael did no more than add to its imagery, the more so as Raphael reached his peak only under the powerful impetus provided by Michelangelo; this in spite of the fact that the two men actually disliked each other. Even the animosity of later artistic movements towards the Renaissance could not weaken Michelangelo's fame and, *sit venia verbo*, his mythologers.

From the point of view of his 'mythology' the vault of the Sistine Chapel represents the culmination of Michelangelo's work. He created this Occidental Pantheon in his thirties, at an age which has often brought to the more fully developed type of man, such as Dante or Pascal, insight into the nature of reality in a form which may be called spiritual or cosmic consciousness.

Working on a strut-frame built to his orders after he had rejected scaffolding made by Bramante, Michelangelo finished the ceiling almost single-handed in four years. Once he slipped and fell from a considerable height. In verses full of bitter irony he describes his physical discomforts during this gigantic task; an understandable outburst, but no indication of his great poetic gift, which will be discussed later.

HEAD OF THE PROPHET ISAIAH
SISTINE CHAPEL

A full interpretation of the Sistine ceiling might easily become too complex. It seems best to consider first the zone of souls with its enthroned figures, and then the spiritual zone with the Mosaic myth of creation. The themes added at the end to the spandrels and lunettes may perhaps betray a slight lassitude on the artist's part and call for less close analysis.

The Twelve. Who or what determined Michelangelo to evoke the seven Prophets, and from some primeval limbo the five Sibyls—

figures which neither Masaccio, Donatello nor Ghiberti or della Quercia could have conceived, divine creatures whose hair and headdress shine more brightly than any nimbus or aureole? Even the aged, white-haired, almost bald Zacharias, deacon of the sacred gathering, bears an aura of oracular wisdom. Did the theologians have a say in this choice? It may well be that they gave the young artist some direction, but it was he who breathed new life into their abstract ideas. This inspiration animates the entire composition within its *trompe-l'œil* frame and we have reason to suppose that the planned shape of the Pope's mausoleum was reflected on the ceiling of the Sistine Chapel. Everything that was discarded or lost during Michelangelo's fruitless struggle for the tomb reappears here in colourful transformation; reborn in the cosmos of the Sistina. We should remember this when we reflect that out of a host of plans for the great tomb in San Pietro in Vincoli all that Michelangelo himself carried out was his statue of Moses flanked by two female figures; but it must be said that the 'Moses' seems to sum up and embody the twelve seers of the Sistine Chapel in one!

Brilliant composition and the use of additional figures makes the Prophets' zone of individual souls extend into the lower, material, and the upper, spiritual, zone. The majestic and at the same time naturalistic seated figures minimize the twelve spandrels and absorb them into their own sphere. Twelve different types of awakened man conform there to a single pattern, expanded by the subsidiary figures beside and above their thrones into twelve splendid variations: perhaps the forefathers or archetypes of the race. What is the meaning of this pattern? Its significance is more than formal and decorative, for with Michelangelo every seemingly unimportant or superfluous detail has a meaning which goes far beyond allegory or intellectual speculation. The throne of each Prophet and Sibyl is raised on a console inscribed with his or her name. Each console is supported by a boyish elemental *telamone;* each figure is flanked by square pedestals forming a niche for the Prophet or Sibyl surmounted by twin *putti* in relief. As a background to each enthroned figure, two small angels are in evidence in varying degrees. Beside the throne of the Prophet Daniel, one of them ventures forward and holds up

HEAD OF THE DELPHIC SIBYL
SISTINE CHAPEL

the prophetic book. A white angulate cornice surmounts the whole design, joining the capitals of the *putti*-pilasters occupied by the *ignudi*. The *ignudi* hold cornucopias, ribbons and garlands of fruit supporting gold medallions in relief placed between them. These *tondi* contain scenes from the Book of Kings.

The symmetrical twin *putti* which flank each enthroned figure are usually a boy and a girl: twin genii or angels. Four youths serenely

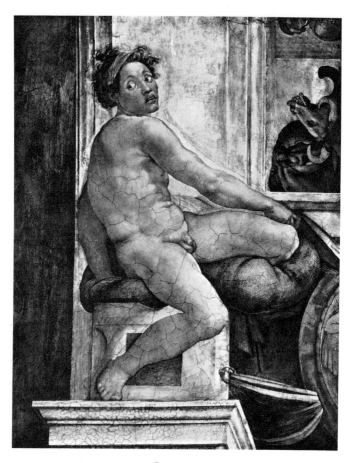

IGNUDO
SISTINE CHAPEL

guard the corners of the five smaller frescoes on the uppermost zone. Thus all the zones are interconnected, giving unity to the host of separate figures. The three groups of supporting figures differ not only by being divided into small children, boys, and youths, but generically. The *putti*, four of them symbolizing the material world, are rather alike; dreamy and idle, unless their function be to act as small Atlases, indicating a further stage of evolution from the dwarfs and nature sprites supporting the consoles. The boyish genii have much more expression and take a visible interest in the

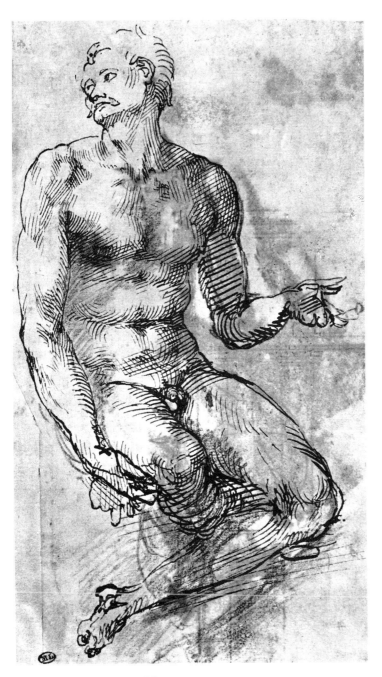

NUDE MAN FROM THE FRONT
LOUVRE, PARIS

HEAD OF THE ERYTHRAEAN SIBYL
SISTINE CHAPEL

vision and activity of the seers. The *epheboi* on the other hand are blissfully detached. It seems right to read into the three divisions of altogether nine additional figures the emanations of physical, emotional and spiritual spheres of influence. The genii in the centre have been interpreted as the two 'souls' in a single breast, the spirit of action and of contemplation; or else a guardian and an evil spirit, which is probably incorrect, although this reading also indicates the contradictions in the individual soul.

HEAD OF AN IGNUDO
SISTINE CHAPEL

On entering the Chapel (generally through the east door, for
contrary to prevalent custom the altar with the 'Last Judgement'
occupies the west wall), one can see the Prophet *Zacharias* enthroned
above. In ecclesiastical tradition Zacharias is young, but Michelangelo painted him as a man hoary with age, with a long beard and an
ample green cloak, perhaps indicative of the unfathomable depth
of his prophecies. This may be the earliest figure; it is extremely
powerful but still somewhat clumsy, hardly suggesting a being who

RAPHAEL. PORTRAIT OF POPE LEO X
UFFIZI GALLERY, FLORENCE

has received illumination. The old man is reading from his book, perhaps reciting the passages on the reconstruction of the temple, which he advocated. Some scholars thought that Julius II and his counsellors took it as a reference to the rebuilding of Saint Peter's. Zacharias prophesied the coming of a king riding into Jerusalem on a donkey, that is, Palm Sunday; and the Descent of the Holy Ghost, the Pentecost—both of which played a prominent part in the Church ritual of the Vatican. A crest with the oak of the della Rovere is placed on the console of Zacharias. Twin genii peer over the shoulder of the Prophet with the book. Zacharias was one of the twelve 'lesser' prophets. Michelangelo chose two more, Joel and Jonah, from among them, in addition to the four major prophets Isaiah, Jeremiah, Ezekiel and Daniel. The remaining thrones are occupied by five of the twelve traditional Sibyls.

The Prophets whose niches are placed in the angles of the zigzag line running from east to west, from Zacharias to Jonah, obviously symbolize a rise and fall in the intensity of rapture and vision; their ecstatic state is not an unconscious trance but a full beatific awareness. Their sweeping movements are controlled and meditative. The same is true of the Sibyls.

In *Joel* the state of inspiration, expressed by the light scroll unfurled like a pennon and the flaming hair, has taken the place of acquired knowledge. The book is under the Prophet's feet, half hidden by the steep folds of his garment. The genii flanking the magnificent head re-enact the process: while one of them closes his book and raptly gazes across the Prophet's shoulder, the other brings his folio and acts as the devil's advocate and the spokesman of mere intellectual learning. Joel's shock is emphasized by a shifting of his body axis to the left. We find this grandiose diagonal movement again in the other giants: in Ezekiel, Daniel, and even more pronounced in Jonah. Joel in particular foresaw the coming of the Holy Ghost, and it is as though he shrank back before the consuming flame by which he none the less longs to be devoured. The lineal treatment of the Roman head—giving it the air of the mighty poet whom the High Renaissance failed to produce—carries to new heights the art form used by Signorelli.

PUTTO TO THE RIGHT OF THE PROPHET ISAIAH
SISTINE CHAPEL

Isaiah is altogether different in character. He seems to listen intently. His forehead may express bewilderment yet he is clad in the green cloak of hope. As he listens, his genii point excitedly into the distance whence the great voice addresses him. The powerful left arm is raised as though commanding stillness or silence. He has an intimation of the mystery of the Son. The naked feet are crossed, and the entire figure expresses veneration, expectation and readiness. What is the significance of the half-closed book which he marks with his inserted finger? Surely, that the book is nothing; books may fail, the voice alone is infallible. Note how the contours of the figure form a circle from which only the head and one hand emerge. The left arm, the left hand, and the head together with the genii, describe an oval superimposed on the circle. The face, with lips parted in expectation, bears an expression of rapt attention; the hair of indeterminate colour, and the vigorously drawn neck emerging from light-toned draperies in blue, green and red, symbolizing faith, hope and charity, indicate that this exalted figure is poised on the threshold of two worlds; it is intent of hearing, it is rapt in attention, and its genius points at Noah's offering. Above the Prophet to the left we see an *ignudo* with a jubilant expression. He and the blithe youth to the right above Daniel prove that Michelangelo—was he not the contemporary of the happy saint Filippo Neri?—was not altogether a stranger to joy.

Ezekiel, the Prophet of the Merkabah, the divine throne and chariot of fire, the heavenly hierarchy and the four cherubim, is shown contorted by his vision. His expressive Hebrew profile faces Zacharias to the left. There is surely some meaning in the fact that this Prophet's head is wrapped in a white turban; holy dread is written on his countenance—the brightness of the vision might have blinded him. The other Prophets are bareheaded, while the Sibyls, like the young Delphica and the old Persica, closer to earth, are veiled or shrouded so as to protect them from an excess of light. The movement of the Prophet's right hand indicates three things: surprise, self-surrender, and the imparting of his vision. Michelangelo thus succeeded by sheer, direct simplicity in endowing a simple gesture with manifold meaning. The contrast of Ezekiel's sombre, heavy garment painted in brown and lilac makes his rapture all the more poignant. The wind of the spirit brushes the fringes on his shoulder. The earth-sprite behind the old man looks terrified, while the beautiful and angelic boy beside him points heavenward with a gesture reminding us of Leonardo's 'John the Baptist' and his 'Bacchus'; late works which Michelangelo may not have seen. But great men who are ahead of their time often express some new idea simultaneously.

To what is the boy pointing? Obviously, to the fresco placed above Ezekiel: the Creation of Eve from the rib of Adam. A connection exists between this event and the prophetic vision, for the first Adam was a heavenly androgyne, a bi-sexual, dual creature, yet a unity; the Neoplatonists were familiar with this concept, derived from the Cabala whose lofty doctrines had been evolved from the visions of Ezekiel by the great Jewish scholars of medieval Spain. We do not know whether Michelangelo had contact with the Jewish Cabalists, though it is possible; after the expulsion of the Jews from Spain in 1492 not a few Cabalists came to settle in Italy. And his contact as a young man with Pico della Mirandola, who was deeply impressed by the Cabala, may have familiarized Michelangelo with these ideas. An affinity with the Jewish myths and visions of the *Zohar,* the 'Book of Brightness' by Moses de Leon, is unmistakable in the biblical panorama of the Sistine Chapel[1].

If Ezekiel saw the beginning and the origin of creation, the first emanation of the Godhead, the youthful Titan *Daniel* knows of ultimate things and of the Judgement which Michelangelo was to paint much later above the altar of the Sistine Chapel. Assisted by his genius half hidden in his lilac mantle, the man who lived unharmed in a lion's den silently sets down in the Book of Life what he has seen. The seer's hand with the foreshortened arm expresses quiet dedication to his task. And it should be said here that Michelangelo's vaunted foreshortening perspectives were never feats of artistic bravado, as was the case with his countless imitators, but always met a psychological necessity or expressed some truth; they are therefore aesthetically satisfying, never grotesque as so often in Baroque art.

It has been observed that the enthroned figures increase in size and volume towards the altar. The bases on which the feet rest become progressively lower, the heads touch the cornice, the hair, hands, feet and draperies overlap the moulding more and more. So as not to exceed the available space, the figures, boldly foreshortened but never distorted, bend forwards, backwards or sideways. The colour gains in harmony and freshness. The colour scheme of the Daniel is astounding in its daring combination of purple, light blue,

HEAD OF AN IGNUDO
SISTINE CHAPEL

cadmium yellow and green. One never tires of the manifold variations in the treatment of the hair and headdresses, especially those of
the Sibyls, and it is worth while to meditate on the symbolism of the
apparently accessory and accidental in Michelangelo's work.

The melancholy, abstracted *Jeremiah*, more than any other figure,
is a deeply moving moral self-portrait. Sorrowful unto death, he
rests from his spiritual vision, to reflect on the hardship and frustra-
tion of earthly existence. We share the artist's pity for this noble

being, prematurely aged and steeped in the anguish of the universe who, alone among the Prophets, must carry the weight of earthly existence. His hand grasps his beard with a saturnine gesture that seems to be second nature to him. The genii of Jeremiah are the strangest of the whole series. The one to the left is feminine and, as it were, an image of the Prophet's afflicted soul, painfully conscious of the absence of pure goodness and beauty on the earthly plane, unless it be in art; and even that was all too often suspect to the zealous among Christian and Jewish communities where iconoclasm was forever lurking in the dark recesses of the mind. In short, the genius is a symbol of Platonism defeated in Michelangelo's youth by Savonarola. Platonism itself found expression in the most sublime

DAVID AND GOLIATH
SISTINE CHAPEL

THE BRAZEN SERPENT
SISTINE CHAPEL

among the *ignudi* on the Prophet's left. The shaping of the limbs,
the perfect torso and magnificent, calmly musing profile surpass, if
that be possible, the Greek ideal of beauty. The monkish, hooded
figure on the Prophet's right is an unmistakable allusion to Savonarola; to the summons of duty and conscience, to the injunction not to
linger unduly in the realms of Greek art. That is why the *ignudo*
above resembles a bent Atlas straining under the weight of his cornu-
copia, bearing a world that casts a shadow upon his shoulders.

This figure forms the greatest possible contrast with the Apolline
youth that faces him. It is deeply significant that precisely here,

above the michelangelesque Jeremiah, on the ridge of the ceiling, the painter has placed the mysterious image of God the Creator issuing from chaos in gigantic travail; a composition which has a surprising affinity with the Chinese ideogram of primeval bipolarity, the *yang* and *yin*.

This God allows the youthful *Jonah,* the seer of Nineveh whom he rescued from the belly of the whale within three days—the time between Christ's death and his resurrection,—to challenge him in his bold nakedness. The figure mocks every law of composition and perspective. Michelangelo conceived Jonah as an Old Testament Prometheus touched by grace, and presents us with a solution to the riddle of good and evil. An artist, himself a rebellious Titan, proffers a solution that spells deliverance in what may be the grandest piece of dialectical theology ever stated in terms of art. The rebellious Prophet, whom God would not have otherwise, looks up directly at his self-begetting and affirming Maker. In his expression, scorn and rebellion are giving place to joy, delight, love and filial response, and the ecstatic contemplation of God. The monster of the sea, the calabash tree of the texts, and the turbulent genii form an animated background, unusually bucolic and idyllic for Michelangelo.

Who were the *Sibyls?* Assuredly they formed the strangest and most intimate link between paganism and Christianity, between the ancient world and Saint Peter's Rome: the projections of an unfinished myth mentioned in Virgil, and adding their lapidary pagan comment to the Prophet's words. Inspired by their gods, the Sibyls spoke in prophetic whispers; they foresaw coming events, wrote prophetic scrolls, and hid them in caves and sanctuaries for the guidance of the people and their rulers in times of national emergency. Since in the opinion of some early Christian Fathers and scholars under the spell of Virgil, Saint Augustine among them, the Cumaean Sibyl had predicted the coming of the Son of Man and all its implications, these prophetesses penetrated the fringes of the domain of Christian theology. Like the Prophets and Apostles, they gradually became twelve in number and were not infrequently portrayed in art. Precisely because Michelangelo's art, at least in its phases previous to the

THE DRUNKENNESS OF NOAH
SISTINE CHAPEL

'Last Judgement', often spoke the language of contemplative theosophy in the older and more enlightened sense, that is to say, of intuitive perception of God, he could not model his Sibyls either on those of Pintoricchio in the Borgia apartments of the Vatican or on any other earlier ones. Most of these, even the Sibyls of Ghiberti on the Baptistery doors in Florence, or those at Pisa, Pistoia, Perugia and Siena, were too rigid and lacking in individuality. Instead, Michelangelo, choosing five, fashioned them according to his own conception, without having recourse to tradition, which in this respect was particularly conventional. His first choice fell on the Sibyl of Cumae, Virgil's guide to Hades, believed to have inspired his prophecy of the birth of Christ in the Fourth Eclogue. His second choice was the Sibyl of Erythraea, because, according to Saint Augustine, she foretold the Last Judgement; next, the Pythoness of Delphi, the Pythia of Apollo, dear to his Neoplatonist friends; and lastly, the Sibyls of Persia and Libya, chosen for reasons unknown to us. On this point we cannot consult Dante who was Michelangelo's foremost teacher. Only one Sibyl figures in the *Divine Comedy,* probably the Cumaean, unless Beatrice in Paradise has become a Sibyl, indirectly inspiring the concept of the Delphica.

Michelangelo may, of course, have remembered the occurrence of Sibyls in medieval mystery plays. But all this is mere conjecture. The artist evidently held fast to his memory of the circle of Florentine humanists, especially of Marsilio Ficino and Petrarch; the Sibyls had been their constant preoccupation. Essentially, Michelangelo's Sibyls are evocations of the departed mother, the wishful dreams of his orphaned solitude; and it is perhaps fitting that in the end, in 1539, Paul III Farnese should have commissioned him to paint the 'Last Judgement' prophesied by the Sibyl of Erythraea, which he completed on the west wall of the Sistine Chapel in 1544.

THE SACRIFICE OF NOAH
SISTINE CHAPEL

THE FLOOD
SISTINE CHAPEL

The unique female figures and representations of the eternal mother are overwhelming. Of course, the Sibyls differ vastly from the Prophets, for Michelangelo remained mindful of the saying 'mulier taceat in ecclesia'. With the exception of the Pythia of Delphi, they are not conceived as priestesses. It is that which is beautiful and most characteristic, in short, their essentially feminine quality, that is brought out. As a group, including not only the three beautiful young women but the others too, they represent the Renaissance ideal of the *virago*, in the original sense of the word;

a woman physically and mentally heroic. One must imagine these Sibyls free of male bondage, chiefly because their male aspect, existing side by side with the female—for they are not masculine women—is very much in evidence in the form of strength and power.

This, admittedly, applies least of all to the *Pythia of Delphi* who shines with a priestly and inspired radiance, which does not prevent this pagan servant of Apollo from being a young and enchanting girl. Whoever has had the chance (as did the author of the present book, thanks to a scaffold put up several years ago for restorations)

to come within close range of these figures, will never forget the expression of this unique being, possessed by her god on Mount Parnassus. Nor for that matter the immediate and overpowering energy of every lineament, often diverging from the traces of the original brush outlines, where Michelangelo's genius guided his hand with even greater certainty in the final execution. The Delphic virgin is coifed with a white priestly band beneath a peacock blue headdress draped like a crown or diadem; she gives true oracles and lives on in the great Holy Virgins of Christian art, who often wear a sibylline expression. The left arm bent over the open scroll is prefigured in the 'Madonna Doni', the fair hair is blown back by the wind of the spirit.

The *Erythraea* (Erithraea in Michelangelo's spelling), is richly dressed and pensively turns the pages of a book, while one of her genii lights a votive lamp. The other echoes her state of trance. It is as though she were under some deep compulsion to rouse herself. The strange headdress threaded with her abundant tresses lends the head with its heavy-lidded eyes a dream-like quality. There is no indication of the Judgement she foresaw. Perhaps its only signs are the scared eyes of the *ignudo* to the left above her throne, who appears overcome by some frightful vision.

The *Cumaean Sibyl* oppresses by the sheer weight of her bulk and a commanding ugliness. With the open folio bound in green and her two genii gazing at its pages over her shoulders she has become one of the Fates, a towering shape with human features. Whenever Sibyls are mentioned, the Cumaea at once comes to mind. In the art of Michelangelo and other painters her powerful presence overshadows every other Sibyl, even her younger and more beautiful sisters, such as the Delphica.

Primordial, totally detached, her eyes focused on things outside this world, and she herself almost a cave of mystery—such is the *Persica* of the Sistine Chapel. Something of Leonardo's chiaroscuro has crept into her composition. She is a presence still more powerful

THE FLOOD. DETAIL

HEAD OF THE PROPHET DANIEL
SISTINE CHAPEL

and secretive, magical and abstracted than the Cumaean Sibyl.

The *Libica,* or Libyan Sibyl brings pre-Christian prophecy to a close. With a graceful movement, displaying her lovely shoulders, her foreshortened arms, and the lowered profile of her fine head with its gold tresses, she lays aside the open book as if about to close it. It is a large and cumbersome volume which might well contain all former prophecies. The splendid and superbly gowned figure is extremely colourful; gold tints prevail in her dress lined with salmon pink : the gold of wisdom, the only certain kind of knowledge. Here as elsewhere, one marvels at the extraordinary effects obtained with the cold, flat technique of alfresco painting, which had none of the advantages and material possibilities of oil. This figure is that of a noble lady rather than a prophetess, the opposite and counterpart of the gloomy Jeremiah. A faint smile lightens her otherwise remote air.

The Prophets and their symbols and accompanying figures are the mainstays of a composition which cleverly divides the wide band framing the Creation myth. They alternate with two groups of illustrative motives whose importance as figurative art cannot be too highly stressed. They are weakened by the unfortunate format of the corner spandrels and the other spandrels and lunettes that cramp them. Their impact is largely lost because of this, and because the lunettes and spheric triangles containing the Genealogy of Jesus are painted in inconspicuous and murky colours. These may have darkened with the soot of candles, or may have been intended to convey a mood of misery and sorrow. If they are difficult to see from below, that was doubtless Michelangelo's intention. The Genealogy of our Lord in Saint Matthew gives no clue beyond a list of names, and Michelangelo was moved to portray the gloom and constriction of human life as a fitting prelude to the sacrifice and passion of the Saviour. Here, too, he nevertheless gives us large-scale figures like Eleazar and Jehoshaphat and unusual devices. Intentionally dramatic and thrown into relief by prismed light are the episodes from the history of Israel in the corner spandrels. All share an uncanny twilight atmosphere: the triangle with the dreadful *David and Goliath*, where the thrust of the sword descending on the fallen giant is the chief protagonist of the drama; *Judith* and her handmaiden with the gruesome burden stealthily leaving the twitching, headless Holofernes; the tripartite episode of *Esther* with Haman writhing on the diagonal cross and Ahasuerus rising from his couch; and the fearful mêlée before *Aaron's Rod* raised up in the desert. The two last-named were probably the last frescoes to be painted and illustrate a tendency to violently massed and foreshortened motives,

THE FALL OF MAN AND THE EXPULSION FROM THE GARDEN OF EDEN
SISTINE CHAPEL

to a ghostly unreality which preceded the stylistic feats of Tintoretto and El Greco, not to mention a host of *dii minorum gentium*. They are Mannerist interludes of fear and guilt, soon to be followed by great insight and illumination.

The contention that Michelangelo, influenced by the Counter-reformation or even by Protestant trends, was 'converted' in later

life, at about the time when he completed the 'Last Judgement', has probably no basis in fact.

To and from what should he have been converted? He was a Christian and remained one to the end. His was an 'anima naturaliter Christiana,' a Christian and medieval soul by definition. But his religious development led him from a pronounced, and at first

NUDE MAN TURNED TO THE RIGHT
PARIS, LOUVRE

EXPULSION FROM TI
GARDEN OF EDEN. DETA

slightly pagan and polymorphous, universalism to increasing inwardness and concentration, to the elimination of every borrowed element, even in his art, until he seems to forswear his earlier art altogether. On the ceiling of the Sistine Chapel, testifying to one stage of his progress, he outlines the deeds and sufferings of the self-begetting and creative Godhead made incarnate in an Olympian race of great beauty and bodily perfection. Was it an act of vanity and pride; a sin, as he was inclined to think in his later years? If so, it was the sin of a devout and beatific mind, and one might reflect whether such self-accusation was not almost a reproach addressed to the deity who is the archetype of the lover and the creative artist, the Father and first Image of his fallen children.

Michelangelo began work on the east side with the Zacharias, and advanced in diagonal bands from north to south because by this means he was able to link up the entire composition; for instance, right at the beginning Joel and his attendants and the Sibyl of Delphi with her satellites opposite are connected by the fresco of Noah's degradation and the four *ignudi* at the corners. He seems to have painted the spandrels and lunettes last of all, adding the mannerist touch of complicated trigonometric corner spandrels at the end. His style became freer, bolder, grander and simpler as he went on. What a difference between the Zacharias and the Jeremiah; between the Deluge and the Creation of Adam! Decades seem to have elapsed between one and the other instead of the two or three years of accumulated experience. The corner frescoes of Aaron's Rod and Esther differ stylistically from the others. They are a prologue to the 'Last Judgement', carried out twenty-five years later, which in a sense calls into question or cancels out all the rest.

The apex of the ceiling, divided into nine fields giving the account of Genesis, is painted in a chronologically reversed order, which means that the Mosaic myth of the Creation profited by Michelangelo's more experienced and perfected style. This could hardly be

THE FALL OF MAN. DETAIL

surpassed, unless in the direction of a deepening spirituality. His late works owe nothing to his personal development or to any aesthetic movement, nor can they be categorized; they are pure symbols of spiritual experience.

Michelangelo evidently neglected the chronological sequence of the Noah series, for Noah's offering should have come directly after the Deluge. Instead, *Noah asleep and mocked by his sons* is the first fresco that meets the eye as one enters the Chapel through the east door. It occupies a small field between the four *ignudi*. But the sleeping Patriarch has surely been placed at the end of the first row of frescoes for some good reason. The degradation of the Patriarch, who resembles a Roman river god, and was yet chosen by God to outlive the Flood and ensure the survival and redemption of mankind, was due not to an overdose of wine but to human loss of spiritual memory; to the hypnotic sleep of man oblivious to his origin, enacted here by the father of the race. The sons who stripped and ridiculed him do not know what they are doing and under-stand neither themselves nor their fate. Noah's devotion and piety pacifies the Father and gives unto God what is God's. For his sake the Eternal has decided to redeem mankind. If the sons mock their father it is their own shame, not his; it is the fall and the inex-orable karma of the race which men in their blindness neither see nor understand. With this biblical motive Michelangelo gives us a blinding insight into his lifelong grief over the human condition. To see in his work nothing but a preoccupation with problems of composition is surely petty and short-sighted. These are self-evi-dent and he solved them as best he could, but his main concern was with mankind and his own soul.

The composition, top-heavy on the right, is not altogether a success. The unattractive way in which the face of the son on the extreme right is outlined is a relic of Quattrocento imprecision which the artist will soon discard. Too little emphasis is given to the motive of redemption symbolized by the Beloved of God digging his vineyard to the far left. The vat in the centre dominates the scene like a nightmare.

The next large field, with the *Flood*, is divided into several sections

HEAD OF THE CUMAEAN SIBYL
SISTINE CHAPEL

with some wonderful details, but these are not properly integrated. Their lack of coherence is partly justified in view of the elemental catastrophe but it offends the aesthetic sense, not to mention the fact that this Flood seems to be a dry affair. One has to compensate by looking at the groups of figures reminiscent of antiquity yet full of new experiments and of movement; of naked human beings toiling, carrying or being borne away and resigned to their inevitable fates. The destructive forces of nature and the elements are hardly indicated. This lack, noticeable in many of Michelangelo's drawings, is a logical one. He sees all passion and torment, all toil and victory in human terms; for him it is not the event itself which is decisive but its effect on those who experience it, expressed in movement and gestures. In their distress men may commit wrongs near the capsizing boat and round the ark, but the scenes of mutual assistance and mercy preponderate, and it is precisely this which raises the perplexing question: why should all these people perish ? It is a great composition but one which still shows the influence of Signorelli and other painters; too involved, full of unsolved problems and over-crowded with detail. The unifying synthesis is yet to come.

Noah's Offering has frequently been compared to classical scenes of votive offerings or sacrifice. And rightly so. But here a new element enters and points towards the future. It is the elliptical composition, partly hidden in the shape of a rhomb, which recurs later (especially in the cartoon by Raphael for a tapestry depicting the death of Ananias, finished a few years after the Sistine) and which was adopted by many artists. This typical Baroque motif has two focal points; unity is divided between two separate poles. The sons of Noah as two athletic acolytes are very much in evidence, while the main celebrant, bending over the sacrificial hearth, is inconspicuous in the background. The unrest of gesticulating bodies detracts from the spirit of the sacred rite.

A bold and momentous step towards greater clarity was taken with the *Fall of Adam and the Expulsion from the Garden of Eden*. It has been noted that the composition's three pilasters, the fallen pair to the left, the pair expelled from Paradise to the right, and the anthropomorphized tree of knowledge with the female tempter in the centre (the Tree of Life before the Fall), join arms at the top to form the letter M in uncial script. Was this intended to be Michelangelo's signature ? To the left, the profusion of the Garden of Eden is indicated by a few details, but even among these a barren stump thrusts up its branches beside the archetypal female. To the right, total desolation surrounds the human couple. The rhythm of the whole composition flows from left to right. Eve grasps the fig boldly, Adam greedily, but in misfortune he seems greater than the woman. He knows that through his fall God, who was near to him, has become inaccessible and remote. He almost disdains the garden of which he feels no longer worthy. In spite of rocks and the barren tree stump, Eden—the term signifies bliss—is too voluptuous and full of delight; the bodies are too plump and smooth, the foliage above their heads is almost too luxuriant. It is as though Michelangelo meant to say : 'This is not yet the truth; that will have to be won in the desert of our destiny.' It is, moreover, striking that the angel with the raised sword pointing the way out, although in flight and strongly foreshortened, appears a twin of the tempter and, like her, issues from the tree (the Tree of Life; the Cabalistic Sephiroth). Good and Evil have divided and become a dual power. This idea, like nearly every fresco on the vault of the Sistine, is full of mysteries which, we now realize, have their parallels in artistic and structural mysteries. Everything connects in Michelangelo's designs. In spite of their intellectual content, in spite of his humbly self-taught knowledge, he never became literary; nor did he think in logical categories or in terms of dialectic, but visually and in symbols.

The *Creation of Woman* is a design cast in simple, powerful form that contains a certain daemonic element. The God and Demiurge, as conceived in the earlier medieval tradition, fills the space between heaven and earth as if about to erupt out of it, lifting his arms with an incantatory gesture and a supernatural air. More is indicated here than mere physical creation: it is the conception of the female mirror-image drawn forth from the sleeping Adam, who lies against a stunted tree shaped like the Staurus, the Egyptian cross. Is he the archetypal son destined to become the Mediator and endure the Passion? The composition forms a right-angled triangle with Adam as the horizontal and God the Father the vertical element, and Eve, in an attitude of adoration, striving towards the hand of God as a diagonal hypotenuse. Theirs is a harmonious Pythagorean unity of spirits prior to their separation. This astounding fresco dominating the centre of the entire vault links Ezekiel and the Sibyl of Cumae, thus underlining the importance of the grand design of the law of polarity!

Greater still and more compelling is the *Creation of Adam*. It is scarcely possible to put into words the impressions roused by this marvellous painting; it is as though current passed from the painted scene to the beholder, who often feels that he is assisting at a hallowed

STUDY FOR A SIBYL
LOUVRE, PARIS

and world-shaking event. Michelangelo experiences the stages of
creation within himself, retracing the way to the divine source by
the double path of religion and of art. Now that, inspired by God,
he has given form to Eve, elliptical and parabolic shapes begin to
multiply; the number of orbits with two focal points increase. As
already pointed out, these were copied blindly during the following
two centuries and became a decorative commonplace. Precisely
here, where man the microcosm and incarnate Word made in the
divine image, the Adam Kadmon of Cabalistic doctrine, issues from
the hand of God as the fingers of the Father and the son flow towards
each other, it is significant and convincing that the Eternal is circum-
scribed by the ellipse (symbolizing the 'cosmic egg') of his celestial
mantle and angelic spirits, while Adam forms only an incomplete
oval. Through the extended hands and arms the creative flash passes
from one orbit to the other. Love radiates from the face of God
and from the face of man. God wills his child to be no less than
himself. As if to confirm this, a marvellous being looks out from
among the host of spirits that bear the Father on their wings; a
genius of love encircled by the left arm of the Creator. This figure
has intrigued commentators from the beginning and has been various-
ly interpreted as the uncreated Eve, or Sophia, divine wisdom. Be
that as it may, this figure undoubtedly signifies beatific rapture.

A divergent meaning has been read into the next fresco by the earlier
biographers, Condivi and Vasari. The spirit of God with the heavenly
host moves above the waters; so they thought in terms of the creation
of the great Sea Monster. But the main emphasis is on the moving
('ferabatur super aqua' in Saint Jerome) and the hallowing gesture;
the title *'God Blesses the World'* is indicated. If we consider further
that the creative spirit advances from the great depth of space suggested by his mantle, which is formed like a gigantic shell, we come
to think of the Waters of the Abyss and the emanation of soul substance, frequently described as a watery element in the mythologies
and metaphysical systems of mankind. This fresco depicts a stage
prior to the creation of man. Three cherubim are half hidden in the
cosmic cloak, as though foreshadowing the Holy Trinity. And, as

CREATION OF ADAM
SISTINE CHAPEL

though he embodied the World Soul, the figure of God the Father
with his powerful hands fills almost the entire space. Michelangelo's
realism, fed on the astonishing symbiosis of the Middle Ages and
Antiquity, perfectly expressed the place, the task and destiny of man
during his journey back to the source of being. His art illustrates

the incarnation of the spirit, free will, and the perversely self-imposed fetters of guilt and evil. However much melancholia assailed him, aware as he was of the flaw in creation, in the Sistina he has contributed to the world's deliverance. Whoever studies Michelangelo's frescoes there does something towards his own purification.

STUDY FOR THE TORSO OF ADAM
LOUVRE, PARIS

On the penultimate fresco of the *Creation of the Sun, the Moon and the Plants* it becomes clear that Michelangelo increasingly discarded iconographic and symbolic tradition. In the Creation of Woman, the Almighty is still standing upright in the 15th-century manner, but here the artist followed his own imagination. This, of course, entailed the danger of a lapse into obscurity and theatrical illusionism; to introduce a simple device from an early illuminated version of the Gospels into a composition treated in a more complex manner

ADAM. DETAIL

CREATION OF THE SUN, THE MOON AND THE PLANTS
SISTINE CHAPEL

was bound to result in an impure style. On this fresco, God the Creator moving above the earth appears twice, once descending with a sweeping rhetorical gesture, and again wrathfully departing. The effect of this grandiose conception is not altogether satisfying. It is forced and lacking in the harmony that Michelangelo usually achieved with substance shown in a state of turmoil. The idea

of uniting the third and fourth day of creation in a single composition was not a felicitous one.

Quite extraordinary and truly Titanic is the last fresco, smaller in
size but sublime in conception: '*Let There be Light!*', with God the
Father self-begetting and therefore, in a sense, self-diminishing. If he
divides the light from the darkness it is the creation and manifestation

of himself as light. This is a strangely abstract design, characterized by primitive and intentionally artless drawing. The anthropomorphous whirlwind in cosmic travail is an awe-inspiring sight. The fresco is Michelangelo's first act of renunciation of his art as a flight into the divine, but he will return in many a lustrum to his tumult of moving bodies which are not of this world, but gigantic images of an inconceivable beauty projected by the mind. The artists of the Renaissance and their patrons were often pagans at heart, but not so Michelangelo. He was the truly medieval man, in whom religious zeal and the love of beauty were at war.

The penetration of nature by the divine spirit, involving as a tragic consequence the fall of man created in God's image, these visions of an archetypal world were placed by Michelangelo above and in the centre of the concrete images of human greatness in eternity (the Prophets, Sibyls, genii, *ignudi*) and of human destiny in time (the Liberation of Israel and the Genealogy of Jesus). The delicate tints strive to suggest the remoteness of these events. He who hath ears to hear let him hear. He who hath eyes to see, let him see these truths.

Michelangelo, forced to become a painter against his will, produced the greatest frescoes of all time and in them achieved the most complete and perfect of his works of art. The sculptures, carried out in what he regarded as his real medium, are more or less dispersed and fragmentary. This raises the question: was Michelangelo's life shaped by his own genius or by blind chance?

Apart from the 'Moses' and the 'Pietà Rondanini', the Creation frescoes and the Seers are probably Michelangelo's most important works. The artist may have produced still more interesting things in later life, when he aimed at an art purged of all sensuous elements, denying himself 'ad majorem dei gloriam'. But his real testament, given before the mystic symbol of Saint Peter's dome, is the image of the heavenly Father surrounded by his children, brought home to us more vividly than could all the Christian theological conceptions put together.

GOD THE FATHER. DETAIL

GOD DIVIDING THE WATERS
SISTINE CHAPEL

THE POPE'S TOMB

All his life his sense of duty constricted Michelangelo, like a ring the
wearer has outgrown. Countless were the obligations he shouldered,
spurred on by his sense of duty; his duty first towards God, then

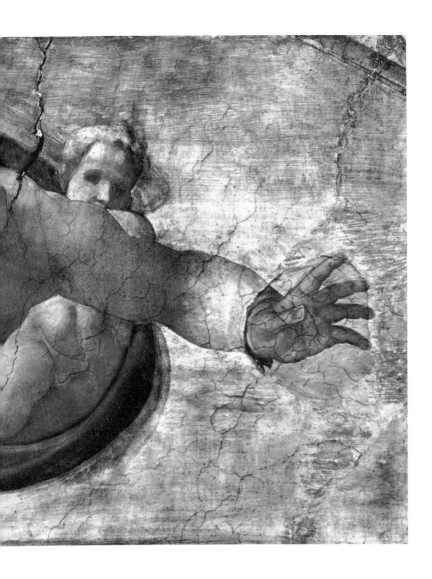

towards his own soul, towards his art and his fellow men. The total
sum of these duties often exceeded his physical and moral strength.
One obligation in particular irked him and overshadowed his existence for several decades; the order for the mausoleum of Julius II,
now withdrawn and now renewed, changed about, causing trouble

between him and his employer and therefore perplexity and economic worry. The final form of the Pope's tomb was to be a compromise. Or was it?

During the night of 20th February 1513, not long after the completion of the Sistine Chapel ceiling, Pope Julius II died, fully conscious and enveloped in a deep sadness. A potion of powdered gold administered during his death agony had proved useless. He was embalmed, which was without precedent among the earlier Popes. Michelangelo must have felt quite lost without his great master, the planner of his Roman activities. The extroverted, pleasure-loving Medici Pope Leo X, who succeeded to the Papal throne, found Michelangelo too overpowering and *'pesante'* for his liking; the cheerful Raphael was a better companion. Therefore he did not employ Michelangelo in Rome but sent him back to Florence, to carry out some architectural innovations in the church of San Lorenzo. But what was to become of the mausoleum over which the previous Pope, more interested in living than in dying, had procrastinated so many times? Even his exhausting and intensive work in the Sistina, which cut Michelangelo off for years from the outside world and caused him to age prematurely, had not banished this obsession. The sculptor in him yearned to give three-dimensional expression to his sense of the earnestness of life and his striving towards a state of grace; for this purpose a tomb monument would have afforded the ideal opportunity. Unborn sculptures slumbered within the marble blocks forgotten by the thieves in Saint Peter's square. Was it a kind of madness that possessed him? Hardly that. In every age, there are men who are conscious of the paradox of existence. They sense how in each one of us an animal, earthbound ego is joined to an angelic self in an incompatible union. Forever, one half must dominate the other, either the animal or the angel taking control. This conflict demands ceaselessly to be resolved. Whenever a decision has been taken by one half of this psychological centaur, it is immediately challenged, and if possible reversed by the other. And from this struggle arise all the problems of human existence. It is the fundamental theme of Michelangelo's art. He had the makings of a penitent and ascetic; in the control of his dual nature he saw proof of a guilt to be erased in faithful service. He wished to bear his burdens and perform his duties, even if they tormented and threatened to crush him. He suffered from an overpowering sense of guilt, and from the awareness of having betrayed his divine origin by his inclination to a sensual and mundane mode of life and by his voluntary exile from grace. In spite of the triumphant Renaissance, he remained a Christian at heart, the son of a race which had produced Saint Benedict and Saint Francis. During his work in the Sistine Chapel, he had become a recluse among artists. Within a stone's throw of the warlike and voluptuous Papal Court he lived a hermit's life. His work was a form of penitence and to this day has a charismatic effect on the beholder. But in spite of his seclusion Michelangelo was far from being free from earthly passions, especially those of a political and erotic nature. In this he resembled his spiritual brother Dante far more than those weird radical saints who must remain unintelligible to most of their fellow human beings.

And yet he dissociated himself strongly from the evil tendencies of his age. The reaction against the Renaissance initiated by Jakob Burckhardt, Walter Pater, Count Gobineau and others has resulted, as is usual in such cases, in our rejecting what is good as well as what is superfluous; rejecting, that is to say, the genuine values of that age, its nobility, unselfconsciousness, freshness and its very real achievements. In spite of our great debt to him, and against our better judgement, appreciation of Michelangelo was bound to suffer from this attitude. And yet this was the man who aspired to beauty and created it, aware that with truth and goodness it forms a triple expression of divine splendour; who observed with an eagle eye the contradictions of his times, the general indifference and godlessness, superficiality and imprudence, sloth and blasphemy. He was the only one among his famous contemporaries to sense the inferno behind the splendid façade.

Although malformed, with protruding squint eyes, and suffering from a malodorous disease, the new thirty-seven-year-old Medici Pope was a man of happy disposition, full of charm, easy to get on with, and in this respect the heir of his more energetic and dangerous father Lorenzo. Giovanni de' Medici, although a cardinal, was ordained a priest and bishop only just before his election to the Papacy as Pope Leo X. He was a man who loved elegance and luxury, comfort, music, humanist company and witty conversation no less than did his father before him. Michelangelo did not fit into the lavish Papal household which swallowed up vast sums of shrove money and 'Saint Peter's pence'. Diametrically opposed to the war-like policy of his predecessor, Leo X soon came up against the della Rovere and obviously took no interest in the mausoleum for the Condottiere-Pope. He did not, however, hinder Michelangelo from carrying on with his plans. He was far too well bred and polite to do that, and his Medicean dedication to the arts compelled respect for the genius of Michelangelo. But his hesitant régime caused the grandiose scheme for a gigantic tomb with a host of figures to make way for a new one on a more modest scale. As time went on, work on the Papal monument got bogged down once more; the artist allowed himself to be sent to Florence, to work as an architect on the Medici church of San Lorenzo and its annexe.

Michelangelo now signed a contract with the della Rovere in which he pledged himself to finish all impending works, not to undertake new ones, and to accept 16,500 ducats as a fee. He rented a house near the Macello dei Corvi, in a gloomy and dirty part of Rome, and stored his materials there. Three masterpieces date from that time.

The two great compositions of his prime, the vault of the Sistine Chapel and the tomb of Julius II, meant that the artist had to encroach on the field of architecture and begin to think in terms of space and volume, and in consequence to subordinate his carved or painted figures to an over-all architectural plan. The architect dormant in him, presumably first roused by his friend the excellent architect Antonio da Sangallo, came more and more to the fore. Although he never ceased to be a sculptor, Michelangelo's gradual development as an architect is an essential part of the story of his life. But in the end he came to regard the human individual as the word incarnate through his poetry, and living macrocosmic mankind as temple and domed church through his architecture. For us to

TOMB OF POPE JULIUS II. 1505-42
SAN PIETRO IN VINCOLI, ROME

visualize man in this way may well be difficult because the idea is too sublimely simple for the limitations of the analytical mind. Michelangelo is known to have said, 'It is certain that the parts in architecture correspond to the limbs of the human body'. But let us not anticipate; the precept of seeing the cosmos and the starry heavens as the manifestation of the divine in Man, and of projecting this idea symbolically into the cupola of Saint Peter's will become clearer as we probe more deeply into his being.

With what purpose did Michelangelo hand the architectural and ornamental plans of the Julius tomb to Antonio da Pontassieve? Did he in fact delegate the planning of the panel tomb to another man or did he merely have him carry out his own design? No doubt Michelangelo adhered to his own plans, but the technical part, the actual carving would have been too great a waste of precious time. The fact was that Michelangelo, usually so insistent on finishing everything himself, and normally in this respect as fatally stubborn and impractical as Frederick II of Prussia and Napoleon, came to realize what he had refused to admit in the Sistina; namely, that he could no more finish the tomb of Julius II singlehanded than he would later be able to finish the Medici Chapel or Saint Peter's.

The altar tomb originally destined for the tribune of Saint Peter's, an architectural grave mound in which we must imagine the sarcophagus of the deceased Pontiff, became a panel tomb of two storeys. Initially Michelangelo visualized it, not in two dimensions but extending in depth and built to hold a good many, if not all, of the originally planned forty statues. It is impossible to disentangle the history of all these plans, sketches and alterations. Of the original statues, the Moses alone found a place in the final version. The others were given away or lost; those that have come down to us, at the Louvre and in Florence, remind us of a great conception that never materialized. After the idea for an altar tomb had been abandoned, the design for a panel tomb was submitted in 1513. This drawing, now in Berlin, is doubly illuminating. It proves the identity of the basic idea with the hieratic order set out on the ceiling of the Sistine Chapel. Moreover, it contains the embryo of the cenotaph of San

Pietro in Vincoli although the final design of 1542 is but a pale reflection of a splendid vision.

In the pyramidal plan of the tomb Michelangelo developed and perfected his ideas and intentions first laid down in a design of 1502. If there the three realms experienced and traversed by the soul—its own central realm, the material or lower realm ruled by destiny, and the heavenly realm above—were designed to show the lower world occupying a wide area, the central world of the soul a smaller one, and the upper, heavenly world a comparatively minute one, the design of 1513 is much more balanced. The pyramid has become taller and steeper; it resembles an obelisk. The artist aims at a greater all-over visibility and clarity intended to convey his spiritual and intuitive perceptions.

Indicated by six fettered, or should we say exiled, youths who writhe like Atlases beneath the weight of rigid herms, the lower storey symbolized the sphere of conflicting forces and bondage. Virtue and vice were meant to fill the niches of the base. This level indicates the world of tribulation and perpetual judgement; in short, our earthly level, and it is hard to imagine how Vasari could interpret the figures as the provinces subjected by Julius II. The meaning of the lower storey corresponds to that of the frescoes in the spandrels and lunettes in the Sistine Chapel, with the care-laden ancestors of Jesus.

The lower section of the upper storey compares with that of the Prophets and Sibyls in the Sistina: it encompasses the realm of the inwardly liberated soul where contemplation has replaced dependence and thraldom to nature, and sanctified action the earlier struggle and rebellion. The two are like the systole and the diastole, joined and personified by the two poles, Saint Paul and Moses. Only the Moses was carried out and has come down to us, to become in the end the monument's sole protagonist.

Because the spirit explores every domain, including the depths of the Absolute, the heavens open in the so-called 'cappelletta' of the highest level. They are made manifest to the blessed and intelligible beings of the middle world as the Madonna descending, borne on the wings of angels: the angels who guard the catafalque of the deceased

HEROIC CAPTIVE. 1513-6
LOUVRE, PARIS

DYING CAPTIVE. 1513-6
LOUVRE, PARIS

Pope. This is the sphere of glory above the sphere of grace, inter-penetrating and therefore architecturally and vertically connected with it, so that the tomb seems to comprise two storeys only.

These new designs profoundly influenced architecture from that time on. We have only to remember the horizontal divisions on the façade of Baroque church and palace, where the lower storey serves as a base for the topmost one and both are joined by a row of pilasters, which in turn might be broken up into additional storeys. Bernini's grandiose Palazzo Odescalchi in Rome is an example.

We have analysed in detail the Berlin sketch since it testifies to Michelangelo's inspired mind and his masterly insight into meta-physical structure. But this plan, too, was never realized. Besides the 'Moses', only two 'Slaves', now in the Louvre, were completed. The lower storey of the cenotaph in San Pietro in Vincoli does, however, bear a certain resemblance to the Berlin design.

It seems strange that Michelangelo should have set aside the statues of the 'Dying Captive' and the 'Heroic Captive', allegedly because they were too large for the final version of the sepulchre. Since these figures, and especially the 'Dying Captive', are unique among his works, one might have thought the artist would have fitted his plans to suit them, all the more so as the 'Moses,' added last of all and dating from the same period, was also a monumental figure, and in spite of many differences shows some similarity of style. How tame by comparison with these two young men, this pair of Dioscuri banished to endure the miseries of an earthly destiny, are the statues of Rachel and Leah, both of them late and probably not finished by the master, although their artistic merits cannot be denied. Obviously the reason for this substitution must have been spiritual and religious rather than diplomatic or aesthetic. We may never solve this riddle, one of many in the life of the ascetic artist; but a possible explanation is that as from a certain time in his life, beginning perhaps shortly before he began work on the Medici Chapel in Florence, Michelangelo no longer wished to portray the hopelessness and despair of earthly life before and outside the final judgement; especially not in conjunction with Beauty, the daughter of Heaven. Such a decision concerning the symbolic content of

MOSES. 1513-16
SAN PIETRO IN VINCOLI, ROME

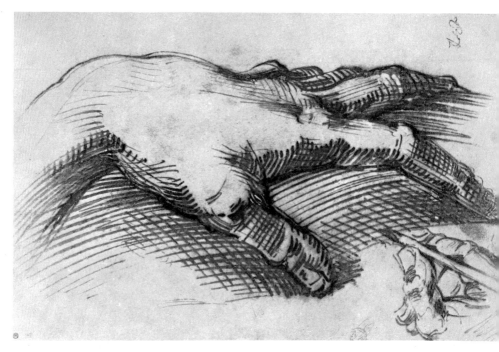

STUDY OF A HAND

his art seems to indicate that Michelangelo's faith had become a conviction. We may be justified in thinking that he stopped work at that moment on the *'prigioni'* (as he calls them in his poems, which are dealt with later). Melancholy never left him, but he had become free of doubt. As everything he did was a form of self-expression, and despair begins with doubt, he could no longer portray despair. And there were other considerations.

Condivi was the first to speak of the *'tragedia della sepoltura'*, and Michelangelo wrote in a letter of October 1542: 'In bondage to this tomb I saw my whole youth wasted.' The strange drama, which had neither tragic nor comic ending but petered out in indifference, is like a gauge indicating the stages of Michelangelo's self-laceration. Basically, he was less tortured by his employers than by his own states of mind. It is almost as though the tomb affair pursued him with a kind of death-wish. Obviously, melancholy brought him to this point, as it did the shy poet Giacomo Leopardi who has much affinity with him and who, identifying his melancholia with '*l'infinito*' was to write: 'To drown in this ocean is sweet to me' ('*E il naufragar m'è dolce in questo mare*'). To this melancholia Michelangelo sacrificed the children of his imagination, 'slaves' and 'prisoners', and the most beautiful among them, the 'Dying Captive'. He almost willed the tomb not to succeed, and in the end denied his art, as Abraham did his son, and offered it to God. In doing so he gave up something to which he had been faithful all his years: the cult of beauty and his enthusiasm for classical antiquity, strengthened by his friendship with the humanists of Florence, and especially the noble architect Giuliano Sangallo, a first-rate connoisseur of the antique and a man of faultless taste. He had brought Michelangelo, probably at the latter's own request, to Rome and to Pope Julius, and introduced him to the latest classical excavations.

Proportion and movement in an animated human body, primarily in the spirit of Greek and Roman sculpture, were always a source of inspiration to Michelangelo; never more so than while working on the Pope's tomb. That is why he created the *epheboi* who had occupied his Platonic imagination for years; yet in the end he removed them altogether. They have survived as astounding isolated works of an artist who was able to conjure up the beauty of Antiquity that time and every sort of iconoclasm had destroyed, investing it with an integrity of a kind to which it had perhaps failed to aspire in its original form. This final achievement of perfection was due to the spirit of the Middle Ages; to the fusion of love and charity, of heart and intellect which lay deep down in Michelangelo's being and late in life blazed forth as an intense love of God without further need of the old mediators, the beautiful pagan deities with their grace and charm. This basic trait of Michelangelo's was obscured and distorted by the eccentricities of his strange and difficult character; especially by an abnormal sensibility, by excessive pride and morbid touchiness over offences sometimes more imaginary than real. Here we have but a manifestation of the wretchedness of human life that spares not even the greatest among men. The darker aspects of

Michelangelo's character should not worry us unduly; the splendour and superhuman quality of his achievement betoken a soul without equal, and compensate for every flaw, every trace of inferiority.

An examination of the two *epheboi* of Paris, and above all the 'Dying Captive', show exactly what the master intended and achieved, and what he wished to eliminate later for reasons that are hard to fathom or approve. In 1542, three years before the final unveiling of the tomb, he declared that these statues were not suitable for it, and gave them away to Roberto Strozzi, a banker of Rome and Lyons, a Florentine *émigré* and enemy of the Medici, to whom Michelangelo was indebted for his care during a severe illness. The Strozzi took the precious figures to France, where they came temporarily into the possession of King Henri II and Cardinal Richelieu, ultimately ending up in the Louvre.

Michelangelo never depicts nature and the body; he depicts the *essence* of nature and the body. The 'Dying Captive' is not dying; he is the essence of death. This is no mere play with words and it is far from expressing everything contained in this sculpture, which embodies the essence of life as well as the essence of death. Perhaps this harmonious counterpoise is contained in the way the arms move, forming, as it were, two triangles: that formed by the raised arm held up to support the drooping head suggesting eternal sleep; and that formed by the right arm, pointing downwards, suggesting a fading and passing away, which yet seems arrested and cancelled out by the lassitude of the gesture.

The unique quality of the statue lies in the fact that while the youth gives the impression of standing still, as if fettered, he seems at the same time to be moving on with an undulating gesture full of gentle restraint, the final effect being one of peace. How was this effect achieved? Surely by investing the statue with such a degree of balance and proportion, that an Apolline, Olympian, classical and not merely a Neoclassical beauty resulted. Thereby it is made to possess an astonishing resemblance to the Laocoön or the torso of

MOSES. DETAIL

the Beldevere, which it surpasses. At the same time it is different from these and greater than either. It does not conform to the classical canon. Here is a totally new concept of beauty, and the secret lies in Michelangelo's mastery of the principles of anatomy and physical proportions. We come nearer to a proper understanding of it if we look for dynamic rather than static values; a revived medieval quality infused into the Renaissance which Michelangelo and those he influenced brought to maturity and which led to unsuspected heights where labels like Mannerism or Baroque are inadequate. One is tempted to say that both Mannerism and Baroque are crumbs fallen from the table of this unique genius.

The new beauty in Michelangelo's works is, as it were, of a musical and polyphonic kind. It is surely significant that Christian religious music began its soaring flight during his lifetime; Josquin de Près, then Palestrina and Roland de Lassus (Orlando di Lasso) were his contemporaries. The Greeks did indeed make music (pre-Christian Rome may not have), but this music was presumably homophonic and monodic, limited by number and metre. Little is known of it in spite of rumours of Pythagorean teaching in harmony. But we can see that in the images of the gods, Hermes, Apollo, Pallas Athene, and Aphrodite, each one is tuned to a single note. Every deity, every note is different. If all these notes together constitute the divine, it is still no more than an imitation; for Zeus, the Father of the Gods, sounds his own note, the peal of thunder. These gods are therefore monodic. Their sum total does not produce monotheism or its counterpoint. In Christianity alone we find one polyphonic God surrounded by monodic saints in each of whom vibrates the entire divine polyphony.

As a true Christian, Michelangelo, even in his youthful pagan moods, gave to each of his figures the polyphony of a Christian concept of God. His is a polyphony of eternal voices. All his artistic precursors had had intimations of the polyphonic human incarnation of the divine but, apart from Leonardo, Michelangelo was the first to realize it repeatedly in his art. This is his unique gift to western civilization. In order to grasp it one must think in terms of musical harmony. The 'Dying Captive' of the Louvre is an excellent example of this polyphony; more than any other work it expresses the inner complexity of fallen man created in the divine image, who, by throwing off the pain of life and enduring the pain of death, is born again in the spirit and in truth.

Apart from the rough supporting block, the whole figure has been carefully finished (unfortunately the left nostril is damaged). It is faintly reminiscent of the *ignudi* in the Sistina but surpasses them in spiritual significance, an achievement which those who have not seen the figures at the Louvre might find it hard to believe. And yet Michelangelo did surpass himself again and again. The 'bungled' 'Pietà Rondanini' was to outshine all his previous works in spiritual beauty, because of his abandoning the more sensuous aspects of his art—and in spite of it.

The 'Dying Captive' is linked at the base with an unfinished shape which at first sight looks like an unhewn block or tree stump, but which is in fact a monkey; barely discernible but unmistakable. The bizarre addition has called for the most diverse interpretations, such as the one which saw in it an allegory of purely imitative art aimed at Leonardo da Vinci. But the monkey who seems to hold a mirror —this is not quite discernible—is part of the general conception of the statue and a gesture of self-mockery on the artist's part. It is probably intended as a mask of earthly vanity; an absurd nightmare which aspiring man must overcome by dying, by casting off his illusory existence and being reborn in the light of truth: the idea is Platonic and Christian in origin.

The other slave, with the powerful if roughly hewn head, the rebellious 'Heroic Captive', is a defiant athlete; a Samson or Prometheus. Here the artist was carried away by technical bravura alien to his usual anti-naturalistic style. This rebel is not Lucifer; he is nothing but a slave filled with the resentment of that caste; a bundle of muscles motivated by instinct and at best a kind of Spartacus. The influence of Hellenistic art and classical Baroque is more obvious than in the 'Dying Captive'; one is reminded of the gladiators in the Belvedere, but even more of the reliefs of fettered and vanquished enemies on the triumphal arches of Rome. This struggling figure was planned as the left pilaster of the tomb, to be seen sideways and in profile. Its technical expertise and forcefulness are admirable. It is less carefully finished than its counterpart and seems a relapse into the *gigante* period of Florence, but without the swagger and with a certain pathos. Unfortunately the stone is cracked across the face and shoulders.

The slave was a grim preliminary exercise for the prodigious 'Moses'. A sentence Michelangelo wrote on 16th June 1515 has been taken as referring to the latter: '*Mi bisogna fare sforzo grande questa state di finire presto questo lavoro*' ('This summer I must make a great effort to finish this work quickly'). Stylistically, the 'Moses' can be classed neither much earlier nor much later. The question arises whether Michelangelo did not occasionally add a few touches to the 'Moses' subsequently, when this statue stood about in his house for several decades. He might have done so during the period prior to embarking on the 'Last Judgement' in 1532, after he had got to know the Roman nobleman Tommaso Cavalieri and felt encouraged by this influential friendship to give up his Florentine connection and settle permanently in Rome.

It is impossible to ignore the fact that, apart from a few unavoidable indications, landscape is excluded from Michelangelo's compositions. The usual explanation that he was primarily a sculptor whose main concern was the human figure is the correct, but not the complete answer. He does not start with the idea of the outer and accidental human being, more or less incomplete and distorted, but with an idea, an image inherent in himself, an intuition or recognition of divine likeness. In his view—a Christian one influenced by Neo-platonism—God created man in his own image as the crown and epitome of the universe. While some people have an inkling of their true being, the large majority shut themselves off and understand nothing. Now an artist came on the scene who knew, who formed magnificent human bodies which were not the reflection simply of arbitrarily chosen models and contemporaries, but images of the divine universal Adam (the Adam Kadmon of the Cabala), having all his completeness; his existence on many levels as world and land-scape, encompassing lights, clouds, seas, rivers, mountains, and shadow animals and plants. Looking deeply into man's inner world we

GIULIANO BUGIARDINI. PORTRAIT OF MICHELANGELO
CASA BUONARROTI, FLORENCE

RACHEL.
DETAIL OF THE TOMB OF JULIUS II

LEAH.
DETAIL OF THE TOMB OF JULIUS II

find all these things. And looking out at the world of nature we see the reflection of all that is in man. Landscape of this kind is not absent from Michelangelo's work. His figures are so rich; their limbs, gestures and expressions, the folds of their garments and their streaming hair reflect and symbolize the whole world of nature. Michelangelo is not the only artist able to achieve this effect. During his lifetime there were others who resembled him in that respect. We think of Leonardo and Giorgione, and especially of one other, born in the same year as himself: Matthias Grünewald, whose men seem like landscapes and whose landscapes are like living men.

Looking tentatively at Moses, the lawgiver of Israel, as Michelangelo saw him, one realizes that the sculptor was filled with the desire to release the spirit imprisoned in a mountain by blasting and carving away the inessential. This fantastic thought came to him during his stay in the Carrara mountains where he had been several times to purchase marble for his Julius tomb. In fact, his Moses is more than a man. He is the spokesman and herald of the 'Ancient of Days', with whom he was allowed to consort as a friend, even though the Lord appeared to him hidden in the burning bush. This, and his entire life's history, his destiny and that of his chosen people are expressed in the peerless figure. It is simply an image of Mount Sinai and of the laws pronounced by God; nothing less than a simile of his eternal presence.

This unique and ambiguous figure, betraying more self-will on the artist's part than any other, in spite of his sterling self-discipline, is the only sculpture by Michelangelo in which he draws consciously on a great original; it still has affinities with the solemn monotone of the high Middle Ages but attunes it to versatility and the contrasts —prolific, but always boldly harmonized—of his own work. Here is a Moses who is both active and contemplative. The work that inspired the 'Moses' was by the young Donatello, finished almost a century earlier; the 'John the Evangelist' in the Duomo of Florence. Seeing this great saint, one might think that Michelangelo created the lawgiver of Sinai not in Rome, but later on in Florence, in close promixity to the Quattrocento model. But one must remember

STUDY OF A MAN
MUSÉE DE POITIERS

that he had a prodigious memory; once he had seen a sculpture he never forgot it. Donatello in turn had modelled himself on medieval sculptures of enthroned Prophet-figures. He conceived the Evangelist hoary with age; enthroned, his symmetrical and erect body seen from directly in front. But the face, framed by dense locks and a flowing beard, and with a long upper lip, is turned sideways and wears an afflicted expression. The robe is imposing and richly gathered; almost regal. The hands, the right resting on his thigh, the left holding the Gospel, are a fine sculptural achievement, while the straight legs and feet disappear beneath the spreading hem. The deviations from traditional hieratic symmetry are tentative and timid.

Michelangelo adhered closely to this composition, creating something apparently similar but in fact quite different; a sculpture in front of which one gains the impression of advancing from the foot-hills towards the gleaming Alpine peaks.

About the central perpendicular axis there are two totally different sides to the figure; that on the right, the calm solar side, is almost vertical while violent movement is imparted to the left, or lunar, side by means of humps and hollows. The right leg, clad in Scythian-type leggings and exposed from the powerful knee downwards, rests quietly on the steps of the throne: the left, thrust back, is poised as though the figure were about to rise. And here two contrary impulses, violent movement and rest, are indicated by the draperies flowing as though in the wake of movement. But these impulses seem to belong wholly to the realm of the body.

A corresponding process, expressed partly in gesture, takes place in the realm of the soul. The contrasting movement of the arms is so expressive that words cannot describe it. They are bare, like those of a warrior of antiquity. Though their position is reversed, their attitudes are similar to those Donatello gave to his Evangelist. The right arm upholds the tables of the law and at the same time rests on them. This gesture alone lends to the whole statue its wonderful assurance and oneness with God. The hand plays idly with the long cascading beard. This beard is the strangest feature of the whole statue. The falling locks remind one of a river swirling down with the elemental force of water. The left arm, bent at a right angle, advances sharply to ward off an ominous event—the adoration of the golden calf by the people of Israel. Here, too, the hand comes to rest in the centre and plays with the locks, like a breeze with eddying water.

It is true to say that the head of the 'Moses' is hardly that of a mortal, even if one is aware that the artist put into it something of his own likeness and something of the character of the late Pope. And in the end, he found no difficulty in placing his 'Moses' instead of Julius II in the centre of the mausoleum. No doubt the memory of Roman rivers gods influenced the composition. But in this interpretation the figure has become the archetype, the enduring Pantocrator of the Byzantine world scene, the source and mainstream of all creation. The face of Moses is charged with sublime energy, superhuman intelligence and at the same time with an understanding of the woes and cares of mankind that far surpasses our own. The eyes under the beetling brows, with sharply chiselled iris and pupil, penetrate every husk and outer layer and pierce to the very core of things. Yet this mighty and dynamic lawgiver knew how to keep himself under control. In spite of his oversimplifications, Sigmund Freud was right in saying that, witnessing what the Israelites had done, Moses desired to avenge his God but desisted from so doing. This is not the old vengeful Jehovah of the desert but a primordial force from the beginning of time. The threatening brows spell wrath, but they are also the ramparts of the all-seeing third eye, indicated by the triangular indentation in the centre of the forehead. The famous horns of Moses are said to stem from an error in the translation of the Vulgate which misread the Hebrew expression for light; here they may simply be the dual light rays seen on the oldest representations of Moses, cut in stone. Apparently the Jews of Rome flocked to see this image of their great Patriarch, in spite of the iconoclastic nature of their faith.

If one is to believe the interpretation of the old symbolist thinker and friend of Goethe, Carl Gustav Carus, a long straight nose indicates an intelligent, searching and productive nature and a discerning mind. In any case the head of Moses sends out emanations, lightning

APOLLO. *c.* 1530
BARGELLO, FLORENCE

flashes of the intellect that announce a storm; he is archetypal wisdom and if the back of the head is ominously flat, that is immaterial since the 'Moses' was planned to be seen from below and from the left, which accounts for the disproportionate size of the head and chest. Placed on the first storey, the statue would have the effect of a lightning flash bursting from the profusion of the sculptured tomb, but even where it now stands it still creates this impression on the receptive beholder. The line passes from the right side of the head, zigzagging over the bent arm and across the folds of the robe down into the nether world; the human world. Such a work of art has the power to disturb the beholder; even to urge him to alter his whole life, as Rilke when he looked at an archaic statue of Apollo wished to alter his life.

The 'Moses' was to survive every reversal in the plans for a mausoleum, and in the end became its kernel; thus Moses, buried by the Lord in a strange land, found at last a symbolic grave known to the whole world. But the tomb was not to be finished yet. Immediately after the completion of the Moses statue in 1516, when Michelangelo was in his early fifties, there was yet another change of plans. A new and most successful design was approved, and a new contract, which gave him a much freer hand. At that time the lower storey of the tomb was ready to receive statues, but the feud between Leo X and the Duke of Urbino Francesco Maria della Rovere, who was temporarily deprived of his dukedom, made Michelangelo decide to quit Rome. In Florence a great task set by the Pope awaited him; this was the new façade of San Lorenzo. The prospect of becoming an architect drew him back to his former home.

He travelled with the immense marble blocks of the half finished *prigioni*, hoping to refresh himself from time to time for one task by engaging in another.

ARCHITECT AND SCULPTOR FOR THE MEDICI

Michelangelo experienced in all their potency, pride and sensuality, even envy and avarice—most of the seven deadly sins, in fact. His works show it and his confessions, set down in the form of poems, though these are admittedly difficult to fathom and have been watered down in translation and travestied in other ways. There is no need to ignore his human frailties but it seems pointless to dwell on them in view of the overwhelming greatness of this man in whom resided a monster and a saint side by side with, and both held in check by the artist. During the last years of his life, the artist began to withdraw in favour of the saint. In his earlier days his unquenchable thirst for beauty, especially the beauty of young boys, enmeshed him in strange relationships concerning which this normally silent man was far from being discreet. But all that was nothing compared to the real sting in his flesh; the ceaseless torment of guilt which the Church calls original sin, the loss of divine grace and of a childlike awareness of safety in the Garden of Eden. He felt unable to find the perfection he deemed man's birthright, even in the highly gifted and physically handsome Raphael, and the austere Leonardo whom he almost hated. Least of all could he find it in himself, being at times virtually beset by self-loathing. But in later life he met two persons whom he thought perfect: Tommaso Cavalieri and Vittoria Colonna, both of whom contributed not a little to the relaxation of his tensions.

When he moved to Florence, temporarily at first in 1516 and then, as he thought, for good in 1518, he was very much alone. In the 'Moses', he portrayed his inner self. The circumstances of his life at that time and the decline of the Renaissance threw his mind into a state of turmoil, and of mounting anger, which is masterfully restrained and harnessed in the grand gesture of the lawgiver of Sinai. He left this symbol of his real self to the Pope and the Roman people who trembled before him, and set out for Florence to tackle new and quite different tasks. At this stage, he was weighed down by old and new commissions, although occasionally he complained of having none. Concerning the façade of San Lorenzo he wrote to Berto da Filicaia in Florence: 'I shall produce the finest work ever created in Italy, if God will help me.' As it turned out, fate dashed this hope, and to this day the early Renaissance church with the fine interior has a simple brick façade.

SEBASTIANO DEL PIOMBO. PORTRAIT OF POPE CLEMENT VII
MUSEO NAZIONALE, NAPLES

La Bruyère thought that one ought to speak of great things in quite simple terms. Michelangelo's works have usually been discussed in superlatives, and, indeed it was difficult for people to talk of them in any other way since the master invariably expressed his inmost thoughts in an extreme, though never obvious form. This tendency increased with the years until, at the end of his life, it impelled him to exclaim: '*La mia allegrezz' è la maninconia*' ('My happiness is my melancholy'). He grew in stature until, when he was in his fifties, his achievement in the Medici tombs reached heights that could not be surpassed in terms of art: beyond that, there was a return to God, a silent mystical communion with the Divine, the nearest tangible approach to which was the symbolism of architecture. It is quite true that if these ultimate things can be touched upon at all in personal terms it must be done in all quietude and simplicity. From that time dates the metaphysical phase of Michelangelo's life and the greatest and most exalted expression of his spirit; but before he reached this phase, which combined a conversion such as was experienced by Ignatius Loyola with the ineffable beauty of expression found in Leonardo da Vinci, he went through years of turmoil, mainly spent in Florence. He had always shrunk from expressing his real feelings in prose. His laconic letters speak mostly of commonplace concerns; vexations, money, family troubles and the like. His inspired mind could communicate only though his art and his verse.

In the years following 1516, as he was changing from one half-finished work to another, Michelangelo's mood reflected the general débâcle and the loss of civic liberty and artistic freedom in Florence. That which since the 19th century has been called the Renaissance came to an end, throttled at last by the dreadful *Sacco di Roma*. The 'Dying Captive' embodies something of this agony. The bold and often cruel and destructive freedom of the Florentine Republic was suppressed by the Medici whose rule had little in common with the gracious flowering of culture under their noble ancestors, Cosimo and Lorenzo il Magnifico. Under Pope Leo X the disciplined Tuscan powers of expression gave way to Umbrian sentiment and the calculated allegories of the later Raphael, which were but a form of Neo-classicism. The rule of the Emperor's tutor and chaplain Adrian of Utrecht, Cardinal of Tortosa, whom Charles V manœuvred on to the Papal throne, was a foretaste of worse things to come. He became the pious and conscientious Pope Adrian VI, with no liking for the pagan muses, the last Pope of Northern origin, detested by the luxury-loving Romans who put up with him for a short interval between the reigns of the Medici Popes Leo X and Clement VII. The medio-

LEDA AND THE SWAN
MUSEO NAZIONALE, FLORENCE

crity of Clement VII and the Medici Grand Dukes of Tuscany was replaced by the rigid and bigoted solemnity of the Spanish Court under Charles V of Habsburg.

Meanwhile, Raphael had died in 1520, a year after Leonardo. The *Sacco di Roma,* in 1527, a shameful and prolonged plunder of the Holy City by the Protestant mercenaries of His Most Catholic Majesty, left a deep wound from which the 16th century never wholly recovered. Owing to the Reformation, the crack in the Holy Grail of Christendom, apparent earlier in the schism between the Eastern Orthodox and Roman Churches, became the running sore of the earthly Ecclesia. Instead of being a rebirth, the Renaissance in its last stages was nothing but a kind a pious fraud, a betrayal of aesthe-

THE RISEN CHRIST. 1519-20
SANTA MARIA SOPRA MINERVA, ROME

tic principles. The tension between East and West had been of long standing and now the western world itself split in two; the opposites labelled Reformation and Counter-Reformation gave rise to sharp dissensions; differences of outlook which may never be resolved, unless the 20th century brings a reconciliation.

These religious discords were to affect the ageing Michelangelo who had been swayed all his life by contradictory opinions, including those aroused by the politics of his home country. He had felt drawn towards both parties, unwilling to renounce the civic liberties of the Republic or the artistic freedom granted by the Medici, which unfortunately went hand in hand with political oppression. The free city of Florence under Soderini was no more, and neither he nor Leonardo had been lucky with their commission for the battle scenes in the hall of the Gran Consiglio. His cartoon had been cut up and Leonardo's destroyed.

When Michelangelo began to build, he thought less in terms of space and volume than of architectural structure and wall decoration. Only once and much later did he create a finely proportioned three-dimensional interior, and that was when perfecting the plans of others, notably Bramante, for the central nave and cupola of Saint Peter's. The road he had begun to follow was a long one, and it led him by stages from the architectural sculpture of the tomb of Julius II to the sculptural architecture of the Biblioteca Laurenziana. If the designs for the Papal mausoleum provided almost exclusively for figural and ornamental sculpture held together by a few cornice mouldings, in the drawings and models for the façade of San Lorenzo, architecture had come to preponderate, even where it was to be enhanced by human figures. The sculptor retired into the symbolic world of portals, windows, stairs, pediments and columns (all of which have a metaphysical as well as a practical significance) and although using geometrical symbols, he gave them vitality and emotional content. Consciously or unconsciously true to the injunction in the first Epistle of Saint Peter, exhorting men to be as the servants of God, the living stones in a spiritual house or temple, Michelangelo expressed it in the symbols of his art (and every form is a symbol) and in his buildings which, whether ecclesiastical or secular, invariably had the character of a temple; they were never an engineering feat but an incarnation in stone.

Architecture, like music, is a more direct incarnation than painting, sculpture, and even poetry, which is the Word, but the Word weakened by the poet's emotional and intellectual reaction to the natural world. It is, therefore, not easy to describe architecture, for buildings are eloquent in their own pregnant and impressive silence. We must listen to this silence when coming face to face with Michelangelo's architecture and try to grasp its significance.

All that has come down to us of the proposed façade of San Lorenzo are a few faded drawings in black and red chalk, and a late model in wood kept at the Casa Buonarroti in Florence. This façade reminds us of an antique *scena* wall whose triple doors admitted and swallowed up gods and heroes, and of the *iconostasis* covered with carved saints and legendary scenes which the Eastern Church took over from the traditional *scenarium*, and which divided the profane from the Holy of Holies, like a curtain betokening the realm of the spirit. Michelangelo's suggested façade wards off the faithful rather than invites them. It comprises three horizontal zones divided by a cornice: first, the lower world; above it, the noumenal world with delicate pilasters, pure circles and rectangles, niches and a remote window. Does God look down through it at his creation? On the summit rests the gentle tympanum of the Trinity, infusing the whole composition with spirituality. The architectural forms are all of very ancient origin. Michelangelo, more than any of his contemporaries absorbed and made them his own, treating them in a way which was copied by many who came after him, as can still be seen on any fairly conventional building. He amassed the parts and unified them in a style far removed from the architectural conceptions of the Renaissance which had treated windows, doors, traverses, sculptured details, storeys, and so on as independent but coordinated units, whereas Michelangelo and his followers subordinated them to the whole. The prelude to this architecture is the severely beautiful front adorned with rich detail of the small chapel of Cosmas and Damian at the Castel Sant'Angelo, finished before his departure for Florence.

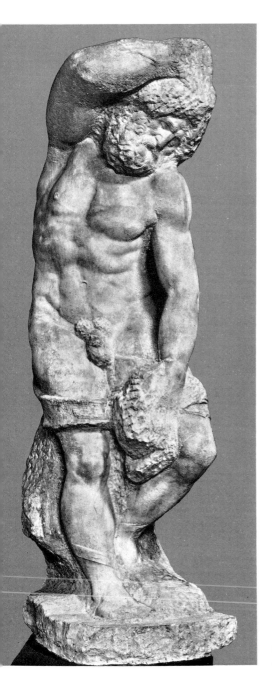

CAPTIVE. 1530-3
ACCADEMIA, FLORENCE

During the planning of the church façade, the master was beset by worries and by other projects. He added to them further by asking Pope Leo X to entrust him with a mausoleum of Dante, offering his services for nothing. A document to that effect is in the Florentine archives. Meanwhile his conscience pricked him on account of the statue of the risen Christ commissioned in 1514 by Metello Vari for the church of Santa Maria sopra Minerva in Rome. This was an ill-starred affair. The marble block, which he began to carve in Pisa, showed an inexpected flaw: a dark streak that passed right through the head of the statue. He was obliged to begin again and sent the half-finished work to Rome, to be dealt with by his apprentice, Pietro Urbano. But the painter Sebastiano del Piombo, Michelangelo's most talented pupil, found much fault with the finished statue, which had evidently been bungled by Urbano. Although another apprentice, Federigo Frizzi, repaired the damage, Michelangelo offered to make a third version. His patron, however, showed himself quite satisfied, and at the end of 1521 the statue was unveiled in the transept of Santa Maria sopra Minerva, to the left of the High Altar. There it can still be seen with an added, skilfully made gilt drapery across the loins. Now del Piombo found some words of praise, but spread it around that the risen Christ was largely the work of Michelangelo's pupils. In fact, several details definitely jar: a certain academic slickness and fulsomeness, the cloying beauty of the head, the fleshy nudity, the cross which looks like a geometrical device—all this detracts from the spirit of religious awe and dignity and from the idea of the Resurrection. This is not a victor over death but a portly and somewhat weary athlete.

The four unfinished *prigioni*, probably dating from the period before Michelangelo left for Rome in the 'thirties' were eventually presented by the artist's heirs to the Grand Duke Cosimo, who had them placed in an artificial grotto near the entrance to the Boboli Gardens in Florence. In 1907 they were removed to the Accademia where they are enthusiastically acclaimed by visitors (especially those who have the present-day admiration for all that is fragmentary, sketchy and problematical). His contemporaries relate that in 1519 Michelangelo was busy with four statues to be finished that summer; they

DOME OF THE MEDICI CHAPEL, FLORENCE

have remained unfinished, and were seen in that state by an envoy of the della Rovere heirs. Stylistically they may well belong to early Mannerism.

Obviously these stone-bound giants, modelled on small clay statuettes such as can be seen at the Casa Buonarroti, were roughly hewn by Michelangelo's pupils working under his supervision. In later years he may have worked on them from time to time until he finally tired of the whole thing, the more so as the 'slaves' were not included in the final plans for the Papal mausoleum.

Interest in these titanic sculptures, which, in spite of being partly the work of pupils, have stupendous strength, centres on the aggressive way in which the artist tackled his material. Apparently Michelangelo always attacked his marble block from the front, as though about to carve a relief, and he made his pupils do the same. The unfinished Matthew, now at the Accademia in the same corridor as the *prigioni*, has the appearance of a low relief. Michelangelo cut straight in without making use of the device of 'pointing'—he did not, in fact, make a highly finished model and then transfer it to the marble. He began with the front and then proceeded to the back view, finally bringing the whole thing together by working on the sides. The back part was often left fragmentary or not carved at all, as can be seen in many of the otherwise finished statues in the Medici Chapel. Michelangelo worked for the eye; he aimed chiefly for a good effect from the normal vantage point of the beholder. However medieval his tastes may have been in other directions, in this he did not resemble Romanesque and Gothic artists who, as it were, worked for the eye of God rather than that of man, so that much beauty inaccessible to those who looked for mere sensuous appeal is hidden in the detail of their carvings. To put it differently, Michelangelo did not tackle his figures from all sides but, working from the front, opened up a third dimension by peeling off successive planes. To the art-historian this technique appears a logical development, for he was after all a son of the Renaissance whose representational style was purely scenic and two-dimensional. That Michelangelo was not consciously anticipating the unfinished effects of a Rodin or Picasso is quite certain. Even Mannerism had no such idea; on the contrary, it strove for subtlety and detail. All sorts of unresolved psychological inferences have been read into these unfinished giants, but these show a disregard for the artist's problem of form. If the head of the so-called 'Atlas' is half buried in marble this is not intentional, but simply represents a stage in his work at which the artist has not yet wrested the whole image from the stone. This need not deter us from appreciating the slightly more finished 'Young Giant', or the 'Bearded Giant', for the work of a great artist shows greatness at every stage.

To modern taste, which tends to ignore the difference between ordinary and poetic language, the unique quality of these figures lies in their suggestion of wonders still locked within the stone. It is surely significant that modern criticism prefers Michelangelo's unfinished works. In these no genuine consummation has as yet been achieved; they are therefore objective and arouse the emotion which Aristotle has defined as a combination of pity and fear: it is debatable whether silent joy in the face of completed harmony is not to be preferred. Tragic emotion and silent joy stand in the same relation as a Requiem to a Te Deum. The unfinished fragments show Michelangelo's despair, which in his finished works is mastered simply by his belief in form and his mastery over it. This conclusion may be unacceptable to an age to which Hugo von Hofmannsthal *(Buch der Freunde,* 1922) addressed his query: 'Is not the despair of the present century due to its lost faith in form?' Those who have lost their faith choose to notice only the artist's despair, which he strove to master, and indeed did master. To think that Michelangelo regarded his fragmentary pieces as finished is therefore quite wrong. From time to time he did not succeed, and the results are abandoned experiments, as the shapeless Saurians may have been abandoned experiments of nature. Michelangelo may have tired of the theme of man fettered: of slaves, *ignudi,* or whatever one may call these Atlases and giants, *epheboi,* and athletes of a twilight period when he swung from pagan to Christian humanism, from rebellion to acceptance and back again. Presumably the theme was not sufficiently concrete. The desired degree of substance presented itself in the shape of a new task set him by the Pope in 1520, to make up for the cancellation of earlier plans for San Lorenzo.

STUDY FOR A MEDICI TOMB
LOUVRE, PARIS

And thus he came to create the miracle of the Cappella Medicea.
He was not destined to complete this either, but as it stands it lacks
nothing save a few inessential and marginal finishing touches.

The Medici Chapel was originally intended as a mausoleum for
several deceased members of the family, almost all of whom, with
the exception of the founder, the great Cosimo, had died young.

TOMB OF GIULIANO DE' MEDICI. 1524-34
MEDICI CHAPEL, FLORENCE

This idea was subsequently abandoned and the builders confined themselves to a funeral monument for Lorenzo and Giuliano de' Medici. Michelangelo began it in the fateful year of 1520, just before Luther read his thesis in front of the Emperor at the fateful Diet of Worms, and, in spite of the ban, split the western world in two. The schism of Christendom was soon reflected in many aspects of life, and not least in the increasing violence and tension of the Mannerists.

NIGHT.   DETAIL

At that time Michelangelo had passed his prime and thought more and more of the life hereafter; the awareness of death was never far from his mind; fear cast him down, hope uplifted him.   His gaze was turned towards the Word and the Light.

We know little about the plans of Pope Leo X for a sacristy and funeral chapel which was to form the counterpart of the Old Sacristy of San Lorenzo, where other members of the House of Medici lay buried: the letters concerning them are lost.   Michelangelo proceeded with the architectural and sculptural plan, thereby proving himself

DAY. DETAIL

a philosopher in the original sense of the term, for the spiritual content of the Medici Chapel is truly inexhaustible.

A careful survey of the interior of the Nuova Sagrestia, which does not harmonize with the exterior of the building, gives the impression of a mixture of two not altogether homogeneous styles, namely a part modelled on the Sagrestia Vecchia by Brunelleschi, and a Mannerist, almost Baroque part. The tectonic lines in dark grey Tuscan *pietra serena* form a graceful classical background to the severe and noble sculptured groups in white marble. Fluted Corinthian pilasters with the buckled corners that went out of fashion in the 16th century, mouldings, sham arches, the circles of the altar area, all this is pure Brunelleschi. But then, instead of windows with Romanesque arches, we have inset windows with consoles, first used by Michelangelo on the ground floor of the Palazzo Medici, and, higher up, tapering windows to add height. Instead of the conical shaped dome of the Sagrestia Vecchia, we have a coffered dome above lunettes and pendentives reminiscent of the Pantheon in Rome, with a lantern whose balustrade and columns foreshadow the more elaborate lantern of Saint Peter's. This is the purely traditional frame for the double niches containing the incomparable sepulchres of dazzling marble, with sculptured groups that stand out like reliefs.

The whites and greys may be classical and cool, but the deeply moving arrangement of the funeral chapel makes one aware of being in a mystical ambience which brings to mind the words of Saint Paul: 'For the spirit searches all things, yea, the deep things of God' (1st Corinthians 2,10).

The figures reclining on the volutes of the sloping sarcophagi form triangles with the statues seated in rectangular niches, who draw heavenward the gaze of the beholder. Michelangelo intended to place reclining river gods at the bases, stressing even more the pyramidal shape of the composition. The outlines of the sarcophagi are repeated in the tympana of two shallow niches placed on either side of the Medici Dukes. Much could be said on the subject of architectural and ornamental detail, but we must concentrate on the essential features of this great work, in which Michelangelo achieved not only his own version of classical art, but the peace and harmony which must lie at the heart of the turbulent universe.

The artist moves with bold assurance from the individual and earthbound plane into the eternal. The statues are not portraits, but images of the spiritual aspect of man. Michelangelo must have known the Medici Dukes, to whom history does not lend special distinction, as men of personal dignity, but evidently saw no reason to leave their likenesses to posterity. He countered sharply the criticism voiced at the time by saying that in a thousand years no one would know what they had looked like. Nevertheless he was aware

TOMB OF LORENZO DE' MEDICI. 1524-34
MEDICI CHAPEL, FLORENCE

that every man is in possession of a divine inheritance, ignored or
imperfectly expressed by him for reasons of sloth, karma, or the
simple fact of original sin, and which therefore may barely show in
outward appearance. As neither of the two Medici was an outstanding personality, the artist concentrated on expressing the essence,
the paradigmatic element in their persons, the eternal self released
in death, of which neither may have been aware in this life. If

Michelangelo had achieved nothing more than this visible metamorphosis of accidental personality, he would still have proved the unique quality of his genius.

Giuliano de' Medici, Duke of Nemours and Papal Generalissimo, was the younger brother of Pope Leo X and husband of Filiberta of Savoy. He died in 1516, in his thirty-eighth year. Michelangelo portrayed this dignitary as an embodiment of the active life, and placed a Marshal's baton in his hand. Lorenzo de' Medici was the talented nephew of Leo X and grandson of the great Lorenzo il Magnifico. It was to him that Machiavelli dedicated the *Prince* ('Niccolò Machiavelli al Magnifico Lorenzo di Piero de' Medici'). Having succeeded the nephew and protégé of Julius II on the Ducal throne of Urbino, he went mad and died aged twenty-seven. Michelangelo turned his paranoiac passivity into a symbol of the contemplative life.

The active and the contemplative; both are withdrawn in eternal contemplation of God. Note that both figures face the Madonna on the wall opposite the altar. The basic idea that inspired the Medici Chapel and its sculptured groups was the 'Eternal Feminine' of Goethe's *Faust*. But before we examine and describe this chapel we must make one reservation: Michelangelo is among the most original and independent men in the history of humanist thought. No balanced interpretation of his genius is possible if we insist on attributing too much to those who influenced his works. In the case of the Medicea, Borinski has spoken of Dante's, and de Tolnay of Plato's, influence. Certainly Michelangelo knew and admired these great minds, but his ideas are independent of either. In order to understand him one has to recognize his intellectual freedom.

The Medici Dukes are seen as beings outside time and its polarity— this is represented by two figures reclining on the sarcophagi which have aroused the admiration of all pilgrims to this Forentine mausoleum. The master placed the statue of 'il Crepuscolo' (Dusk) and 'Aurora' (Dawn) on either side of the figures of the Duke of Urbino,

LORENZO DE' MEDICI. DETAIL

EVENING.   DETAIL

called 'il Pensieroso'. His bent head is turned away from 'Dawn'
towards the genius of eventide, and in the direction of the Madonna
on the entrance wall. Before he lost his reason the melancholy
young Medici, who was something of a poet, had written: 'It is
not cowardice, and is not due to cowardice, if a man distrusts his
earthly fate and longs for the last breath, for even the happy man
knows not what awaits him; it might be unbearable—unfeeling
rock, how I envy you!'

It is as though the beginning and end of the world were represented

DAWN. DETAIL

here, and higher up, in the metacosmos, the messenger of creative
energy. Leaning on a casket adorned with a bat's head, and plunging
a gloved right hand into a leather wallet, he holds dangerous gifts
in readiness. What is hidden there? Insidious gold? or binding
contracts? A lion gapes from the Duke's helmet. This thoughtful
figure belongs to an intermediate world; he has power and possessions.
Does he return them to the world and preserve his soul intact for
the God inherent within him? Much is expressed by the head of 'Dusk'
with its unspoken nostalgia, not for the peace of apparent annihilation,

but for final transmutation into a higher plane of being. In the reclining figures, a wealth of gentle movement is harmonized in the wonderful parallelism of the limbs. Witness the head and left arm of 'Dawn', the head and lower arm of 'Dusk', to mention only two instances among many. The contrast between a clothed and two naked figures expresses the great mystery of identity and polarity; for the three are really identical; they are at once a giving forth and a gathering in, reality and potentiality, the dual creatures of twilight in whose contemplation the Thou and I are merged in one. The fish scales covering the legs of the consoles beneath the sarcophagi indicate that life arose from the primeval waters. As already stated, it was intended to use river gods as the bases of both groups.

The opposite tomb, presumably finished later, is of Giuliano, Duke of Nemours, who like Lorenzo wears the tunic of a Roman General. This magnificent counterpart resembles the contemplative group in composition and detail, although as an emblem of the active life it expresses a completely different mood. Instead of twilight figures, 'Day' and 'Night' ('il Giorno' and 'la Notte') flank the Duke, whose movements are less complex, more relaxed, faintly reminiscent of the 'Moses'. Lorenzo's figure in heavy and elaborate garb seems wrapped in a half-light; that of Giuliano radiates a solar splendour. The bare, expressive hands laid on the marshal's baton seem to vibrate with energy, while the youthful imperial head, turned towards the Madonna, has a dreamy, thoughtful expression. It is as though the warlike elements symbolized by Scythian-Sarmatian masks on his leather cuirass have been externalized, leaving only an inner radiance which contains no elements of violence. One is thus tempted to see in Giuliano the spirit of life and in Lorenzo that of death. As 'Dawn' and 'Dusk' were not extreme opposites, but, as it were, obverse and reverse; they befit the contemplative life, while 'Day' and 'Night' suitably flank the representative of the active life. Are these astonishing figures allegories or symbols? We may call them 'Day' and 'Night', but they are more, and other, than that. They represent a paradox; for the age and female ugliness of 'Night' is truly beautiful, and the masculine, athletic beauty of 'Day' manages to be repulsive. In other words, the overpowering strength of

VICTORY. 1525-30
PALAZZO VECCHIO, FLORENCE

'Day' repels, but there is an appeal in the lassitude of a body tired out by living, conceiving and giving birth. These instances of polarity, too, are aspects of the human ambivalence of Giuliano who appears as the spirit of life. This emblem of action is at the same time meditative, not unlike a neutral General watching an imaginary battle, or a chess player engaged in a game with himself. The 'Pensieroso', on the other hand, is hiding something; he is hiding not only his face but his passions, doubts and fears, and his abstracted attitude contains a disquieting element of aloofness. In brief, all these figures are not only ambivalent, they are polyvalent and are more than mere symbols or theatrical allegories. They lack nothing except the breath of life—and the inability to bestow this is the Promethean torment of genius.

There is much else to see in the Medici Chapel; thrones, goblets, masks, rams' heads, shells, wands; all of them full of meaning and aesthetically satisfying. But one figure remains to be examined and interpreted: the 'Madonna Medici', partly unfinished and placed against the bare entrance wall.

This Madonna and Child, on which Michelangelo worked for over a decade without coming near to finishing it, sums up every detail of the Chapel, whose theme is death and resurrection. She is imperishable Light, feeding the souls here and beyond; she is the *Anima Mundi*, the maternal aspect of God depicted as incorporeal and barely touching the earth. The statue seems a symphonic elaboration of the Madonna of Bruges. The Virgin is truly divine; she holds her child to her breast, like the 'Madonna of the Stairs' but here the relationship between mother and son is no longer an earthly one; it is a universal symbol. A complicated interplay of forms, which cannot truly be called Mannerist, results in a whole that expresses harmony and repose. Although unfinished, the face of the Holy Virgin is divinely beautiful. The figure is carved in the classical 'wet garment' style, but the fluidity of the robe is not that of water; the limpidity of her gaze does not suggest tears. The Virgin seems bathed in some fiery essence; subjected to a baptism of fire. Seen from below, the statue conveys unbearable agony, like Dante's Purgatory, but seen from above—which viewpoint gives far more

MADONNA AND CHILD. 1524-34
MEDICI CHAPEL, FLORENCE

MADONNA, CHILD AND SAINT JOHN
BRITISH MUSEUM, LONDON

insight—it is a pure pentecostal flame; the true representation of a celestial being.

How could Michelangelo abandon such a work? The explanations that he deemed it finished, or found himself unable to continue, do not quite convince. Did he have here his first intimation of a call to abandon art for pure contemplation? We shall never know.

The patrons of the house of Medici, Cosmas and Damian, at the Virgin's side, were carried out by others from Michelangelo's design. He had many more plans for this chapel, for instance a Resurrection for the lunette above the Madonna; but the present work is concerned with what is, and not with what might have been. The 'Crouching Boy' of Leningrad may have been destined for the chapel, but neither this nor the figure's authenticity have been attested.

To this Florentine period belong two further statues and the works connected with the Biblioteca Laurenziana; among these, which may be regarded as further stages in Michelangelo's process of adapting his genius to the medium of architecture, the most memorable achievement—indeed, a landmark in European building history—is the staircase in front of the reading room. Michelangelo made the original design and model in 1558, during his late Roman period. Ammanati and Vasari carried them out twenty-five years after he left Florence.

As we have seen, Michelangelo seems to have been born under an unlucky star, which branded him in early life with a broken nose. If an insignificant bully could inflict this disfigurement on him, it is scarcely surprising that he was frequently overcome by the precariousness of existence, suspecting enemies, intriguers, cheats and murderers everywhere. His father, a provincial official of limited outlook for whom he did all he could and for whose sake he humbled his pride, complained incessantly of his famous son. His brothers, who ill-treated the old gentleman, never stopped extorting money from Michelangelo who was unable to derive pleasure from his possessions. He was continually short of money because out of false pride he had turned down a pension offered him by Clement VII, though he was forced in the end to beg for it to be paid. Chary of accepting unsuitable or poor material, he frittered away months and years of precious time and spent vast sums in the quarries of Carrara and Serravezza. He was convinced that neither his friends nor his apprentices could be trusted. He wanted to do everything unaided, and wasted time and energy in the process. In reality there were many, even in his youth, who sincerely admired and supported him, and throughout his life a series of Popes placed their trust in him. The burden of work, increased by his stubbornness and the frugal life he led, impaired his health and ruined his nerves. If he happened to be free from actual worries, he tortured himself with introspection, scruples of conscience and apocalyptic fears. His transcendent aspirations gave him a negative attitude towards the material world. But these very aspirations urged him to create, and what he created were images and copies of the world of ideas. Gradually, the pleasure and torment of his obsession with work engulfed all other passions. In his old age, his immortal longings were transformed into an inner certainty which caused him to turn completely away from the external world and renounce its symbols. Through penitence and asceticism he passed from his state of torment through purifying flames towards the supreme Light. Whether, like Plotinus and Pascal, he saw its radiance in this life we cannot be certain. But bearing all this in mind, one begins to understand the plan of the Biblioteca Laurenziana and the staircase to the reading room, which has too often been misinterpreted as a Baroque *tour de force*. For Michelangelo more than for any other Renaissance artist, architecture was the supreme means of expressing eschatological intuition.

Michelangelo's biography is to be found in his artistic and spiritual achievements. There is not much worth recording where his everyday existence in concerned; there was no room in it for careful and ordered bourgeois comforts and relationships. In daily life all his energy went into his work. And so it continued until the influence of Tommaso Cavalieri, a young man of genuine kindness and great physical beauty, and of the devout and zealous Vittoria Colonna transformed the man Buonarroti and changed his outer life; thereby it was at last granted him to be a friend and intimate. What he was, knew and aspired to, he had always expressed in his

EARLY STUDY FOR THE ENTRANCE TO THE VESTIBULE
OF THE BIBLIOTECA LAURENZIANA
CASA BUONARROTI, FLORENCE

art. He stated it succintly and without the aid of sculptured detail
in the staircase of the Biblioteca Laurenziana, a conception that came
to him as he stood on a threshold which he did not as yet dare to
cross. Years of comparative aridity lay ahead, of time lost in plans
for fortifications, political disorientation, indecision and hopelessless.
The change of heart came in 1532, after the general depression follow-

ing the siege of Rome and Florence, when he met Cavalieri during a visit to the Papal city in connection with the tomb of Julius II.

The plan for the Laurenziana was conceived immediately before the sack of Rome. It strikes one as a liberating gesture of escape from troubled times, and from time itself; a quiet ascent towards Infinity. At first one is overawed by the solemn, almost funereal architecture of a closed space pressing in on the famous stairs. Jakob Burckhardt thought its walls, closely confining grouped pillars, an 'open defiance of form'. Light in colour but closely packed with dark consoles, mouldings, mock windows, these walls seem to advance silently on the visitor ascending the stairs, like stern and sombre guardians of the threshold. The funeral music from *Don Giovanni* comes to mind and one is reminded that the Spanish army was about to descend on Rome. But the stairs, with their lively curves and volutes speaking the language of cabalistic form and number, spell deliverance from temporal matters. The influence of the expert and devout interpreter of the Pentateuch, Pico della Mirandola, may be suspected here, unless Michelangelo was in direct contact with refugee Jewish scholars from the Iberian peninsula.

The staircase is not merely an idle game or speculation on number and its mysteries; it is a gesture of adoration before the divine Presence and its hierarchies. The three bottom stairs, derived from the Doric temple, symbolize the Trinity; for this Jacob's ladder with its threefold vertical and horizontal divisions embodies the hermetic cabalistic principle: 'As above, so below!' In the topmost section of the staircase, consisting of five steps, the Trinity returns to unity. Five is the number of rays in the aura of the Son of God, the Word, or man made perfect. Descending the five steps, one reaches a small half-landing bordered by volutes, inlaid with a dark ellipse having widely spaced focal points. From these focal points —the bipolar element again—two subsidiary stairs lead down off the balustraded main staircase. With their absence of support rails and their five landings each, were they perhaps intended to suggest, on the one hand the ever-present peril to man of the Fall, on the other the danger of his becoming side-tracked and so inwardly dying? Seven more stairs lead to a second half-landing, and finally we reach

the three lowest steps.   The way up is the way down: it is the way
leading from God back to God, to the Trinity and Crown of being.
These steps symbolize ineffable holiness, and the seven superimposed
Ionic volutes which correspond to the divine attributes and their
'brightness' (*Zohar*—Brightness[1]) embody the sacred number ten
of the Cabala, the Sepiroth and their Christian derivations.   From
our vantage point the strange cascade or emanation in noble stone

is God who descend to us: from the topmost stair He sees it as our ascent. God is perpetual ascent. He is the Trinity and the seven Powers or spirits spoken of in the Apocalypse as the seven stars and the seven golden candlesticks.

The Sack of Rome by the mercenaries of Charles V drove the politically powerless Pope Clement VII to seek a self-imposed captivity in the Castel Sant'Angelo; and it was the pretext for the Republican, and practically anarchist, Florentines to rid themselves once more of the Medici. Michelangelo's work on the New Sacristy of the Medici Chapel suffered a lengthy interruption. When Pope and Emperor made up their differences and decided to reinstate Alessandro de' Medici as ruler of Florence, the Signoria resisted and called on Michelangelo to build new and stronger city ramparts. He travelled to the Duke of Ferrara to seek advice, and in return painted for him a 'Leda'. This, however, never reached Alfonso, and has long since been lost. From two feeble copies—one a painting at the National Gallery, the other a somewhat facile sculpture by Ammanati in the Bargello—we can see a resemblance to 'Night', and lament the loss of what was probably a great painting.

In those years Michelangelo was often disorientated and disturbed, and the few sculptures dating from them are troubled and ambiguous pieces, in spite of their beauty. His post as Governor and Procurator of the bastions of Florence caused him much worry, although the excellence of his engineering feats has been attested. He was indebted to the Medici and had done wonders for them, but now, caught in the vortex of Republican politics, with which he sympathized, he was asked to act and fight against his former masters. During the siege he panicked, fearing death at the hands of General Malatesta Baglioni and, taking a considerable sum of money with him, fled to Ferrara and Venice where he was received with honour. Later, he repented and returned; whereupon he was forgiven, for his help was urgently required. The traitor Baglioni capitulated shortly after, and on 12th August 1530 handed over the city to the enemy. This time it was the turn of the Medici to forgive Michelangelo. Many men were put to the sword at that time, but they did not wish to lose so great an artist. In order to ingratiate himself he began an exquisite statue for the Papal envoy, the hated Baccio Valori who later became involved in the conspiracy against the Grand Duke Cosimo and was beheaded in the Piazza della Signoria. This statue, too, remained unfinished. Michelangelo also pledged himself to finish the New Sacristy. He could not forget that he had humbled himself before the Florentine tyrants and their party. Eventually he fell seriously ill and everyone, including the Pope, feared for his life. The statue made for Valori, which in the inventory of Duke Cosimo and in the writings of some scholars figures as 'The Young David', was an Apollo. Vasari, whose opinions it has long been the fashion to discount, expressly says so. On the back of the statue we can see the rough outlines of a quiver, and the boyish, androgynous god reaches over his shoulder for an arrow, while his dreamy head is turned sideways, the right arm hanging loosely and probably holding a fragmentary bow. The position recalls Raphael's Apollo in the fresco of the 'School of Athens'. The right leg of Apollo on the threshold of his youthful beauty rests on a flattened sphere which might have become the shell of a tortoise such a Hermes used for the invention of the lyre, and presented to his brother, Apollo. The enchanting figure, like an angel lost in our sublunary world, has a nostalgic charm; real affection must have gone into its creation.

At a period when, in addition to every other trouble, he was afflicted by headaches and rheumatism and by newly arisen problems concerning the Papal tomb, Michelangelo began a mysterious larger-than-life group. It was probably intended for the mausoleum, the more so as the main figure is crowned with oak leaves, which appear in the crest of the della Rovere. This sculpture, twisted in a compli-cated spiral movement reminiscent of certain steeples by Borromini, is thought to represent a winged victory. But the conquest it implies has nothing to do with the pride and thoughtless aggression of instinctive man. The semi-nude Victor, who assumes a pose similar to that of the 'Apollo', pulls up his cloak by a cord with an embarrassed and uneasy gesture typical of Michelangelo while looking into the distance with a searching gaze, as if sensing some danger; this Victor's conquest does not please him. It is disturbing that one iris only has

THE ENTOMBMENT. ATTRIBUTED TO MICHELANGELO
NATIONAL GALLERY, LONDON

been carved—in the corner of the right eye. The Victor seems to be kneeling on a bearded, rather indistinct *telamone*, or rather on the burden carried by the latter. Is he Atlas, bearing the weight of the world? Is he a daemon? Or is he humanity crushed by fate, or age, or its own accumulated crimes? Are we to see in it victory of truth over illusion, or virtue over vice? None of these assumptions are quite convincing, least of all the old interpretation according to which Michelangelo portrayed the shame and humiliation of his passion for Cavalieri, who is said to have been the model for this statue. Most probably it was made before he met the young noble-man, and in any case it remained in Florence when he left for Rome. The most likely interpretation may be the victory of genius over the baser self. But one cannot be sure, and this lack of clarity, coupled with a certain affectation, this time decidedly Mannerist in character, leaves the beholder dissatisfied and in doubt. It seems that some change of mind was imminent, a recoil from the painful indecision and deep disgust which must have profoundly tormented Michel-angelo during that period.

At that time Michelangelo shed his patriotism like an old skin. His father had died, and after one of his brothers, Buonarroto, expired in his arms of the plague, nothing—least of all his trouble-some surviving brothers—bound him to the beloved city.

A homeless man, in his late fifties, he left for Rome in 1534. Pope Paul II Farnese, having succeeded his comparatively young prede-cessor, wished to attract the artist to his Court and establish him as chief architect and sculptor.

THE CHANGE OF MIND: THE LAST JUDGEMENT

While it is regrettable that Michelangelo left the Cappella Medicea half-finished, his final flight from Florence was justified; his father and his favourite brother were dead. Open tyranny had succeeded Republican legislation. Duke Alessandro was furious with Michel-angelo because of his unwillingness to build fortifications. The latter's excuse was his obligation towards the Pope, a distant relation

TITIAN. PORTRAIT OF POPE PAUL III
MUSEO NAZIONALE, NAPLES

MADONNA AND CHILD WITH SAINT JOHN AND ANGELS. ATTRIBUTED TO MICHELANGELO
NATIONAL GALLERY, LONDON

of the Duke but too far away to shield the artist from the impudence or violence of an arrogant ruler. In addition to all this, Baccio Bandinelli, a technically accomplished but mediocre sculptor, an imitator of Michelangelo and the author of the almost grotesque Hercules group in front of the Palazzo Vecchio, had gained considerable influence at the Florentine Court. These circumstances drove Michelangelo from his home.

He was attracted to Rome, not so much by professional interests, which it is true, grew by leaps and bounds after his arrival, as by his longing for a friend whom he had met a short while before and by his admiration for this man's perfect physical beauty, noble bearing and moral strength. This passionate and almost childlike devotion was less that of an invert than of an introvert. In his art, Michelangelo had reflected an ideal conceived in his own mind and soul. Now the lonely Platonist suddenly found himself confronted with this reflection in human form. It was thus all too easy to abandon Florence, since life in Rome offered him fulfilment and complete integration. He, who never worked from living models unless it were to caricature them, painted a portrait of Tommaso Cavalieri, whom we may imagine as Plato's Lysis or Schiller's Marquess of Posa. Unfortunately it has been lost. Michelangelo made a number of drawings, which are discussed later, and wrote inspired verses dedicated to his gentle and reserved friend. Cavalieri remained true to him to the end and was present at his deathbed.

Michelangelo's problems of expressing himself in his work are inseparable from his religious and emotional life. During his lifetime, science, until then the handmaiden of theology, had become divorced from religion. It has sometimes been said that, prior to his so-called conversion during work on the 'Last Judgement', Michelangelo was not a true Christian; that he was under the spell of Mosaic-Hebrew tradition on the one hand, and Greek and Latin antiquity on the other. Certain elements of Manichaeism, not uncommon in Christianity—witness Saint Augustine whose Manichaean early training left unmistakable traces,—are discernible; as for Neoplatonism, towards which at times the Church was favourably disposed, it contained elements of Manichaean dualism and shared its doubts

THE LAST JUDGEMENT. DETAIL

THE LAST JUDGEMENT. 1536-41
SISTINE CHAPEL

THE LAST JUDGEMENT. DETAILS
SISTINE CHAPEL

STUDY OF MALE FIGURES FOR THE LAST JUDGEMENT

whether evil, even an evil which is an illusion, could ever be overcome and vanquished by good.

In order to depict the world beyond, Michelangelo invariably uses
the shapes and symbols conjured up by our imagination; this other
world, seen in the flash of immediate vision as in the 'Last Judgement', arouses terror in the unprepared, whose conception of it is
blurred and full of lulling and often sweet delusions. The spiritual
world is not only paradise but a limitless field of energy that
includes light and darkness, saints and devils, eluding our narrow
consciousness which is limited and conditioned by the senses. In
his old age the range of Michelangelo's vision far surpassed the laws
and boundaries of ordinary existence and its limitations.

On 23rd September 1534, the master, then in his fifty-ninth year,
arrived in Rome. Two days later his comparatively young and

ever unreliable benefactor Clement VII was dead. The conclave met and elected Paul III, a Farnese and an even greater admirer of the artist. The new Pope was a highly civilized and intelligent man of sixty-seven; rather frail though destined to reign for the next sixteen years, he was very anxious to attach Michelangelo to himself and make him carry out a project planned by his predecessor under the impact of the dire political events.

On 6th May 1527 the Lord of Christendom, hard pressed by the Emperor Charles V, had been anxiously praying in the handsome Chapel of Nicholas V Parentucelli adorned by Beato Angelico in his clear Trecento style with the legends of Santo Stefano and San Lorenzo—it is of course a fallacy to imagine the Renaissance Popes as cynical unbelievers—when Protestant forces who had broken away from their commander, General Georg von Frundsberg, burst into the Vatican. The Pope escaped by way of a covered corridor to the Castel Sant'Angelo, but the mercenaries recognized his white cassock between the interstices of the crenellated wall and shot with arrows, bolts and cannon balls at the exalted fugitive, who was shielded eventually by a black-robed prelate. Clement VII, though the humiliation of his city was a thing of the past, had planned to erect a commemorative monument. Michelangelo was to paint the Fall of Lucifer and his angels on the entrance wall of the Sistine Chapel, and the Last Judgement above the altar. In the end the idea of the fallen angels was abandoned, and attention was concentrated on the Judgement; it was decided to cover the entire altar wall, without consideration for earlier paintings there.

The commission was confirmed, and soon after his election Paul III, accompanied by a suite of Cardinals, called on Michelangelo at his humble home near the Macello dei Corvi, and approved the preliminary design—or it may have been a cartoon—demanding that his host start work at once. Michelangelo demurred, referring to the unfinished tomb of Julius II, but gave in when the Pope insisted violently and offered to assume all responsibility towards the Rovere heirs. Paul III visualized this powerful fresco as a *menetekel* for mankind, a sort of prelude to the intended Council whose object would be to overthrow heresy and cleanse morals within the Church, without making violent changes. In fact, the Council of Trent called for also by Luther and Henry VIII began after considerable delays on 13th December 1555, four years after the completion of the great fresco, to accommodate which a series of Papal portraits, two frescoes by Perugino, and two lunettes by Michelangelo were removed, and two windows bricked up.

The preparations—that is to say, the final cartoon and the treatment of the wall—continued until 1536. According to Vasari a new wall was built, slanting inward to the extent of about a foot at the top so as to prevent grit and dust from accumulating. It was not very effective, especially against the soot of candles. The fresco defines Michelangelo's religious position as it was before his friendship with Vittoria Colonna, begun in 1538. It keeps to established ideas and formulae which can be summed up as justification by faith and works, among which he obviously counted martyrdom. The extreme Augustinian attitude and the evangelizing doctrine of grace current in Vittoria Colonna's circle had not yet begun to gain ascendancy over Michelangelo's mind. The 'Last Judgement' was finished in the autumn of 1541, and solemnly unveiled at the eve of All Souls. It is the second finished painting by the sculptor who would not be a painter and yet completed nothing but his paintings. Had his Papal benefactors guessed that to inveigle him into painting was the only way of pinning down this restless being?

The painters of the Quattrocento had adorned the wall below the windows of the Sistine Chapel with a handsome band of pictures from the Old and New Testament. Michelangelo overshadowed the exquisite style of these, and virtually annihilated them by the sheer weight of his visions and creations of biblical history, on the ceiling. Now he went beyond this, denying what had been a part of himself, that part which had identified itself with the proud humanism of the High Renaissance. Without losing his mastery of technique, he offered it, in the representation of the Second Coming, to the Judge, together with all his ideas of aestheticism. In his silent renunciation of humanism he acknowledged that society was embarking, and indeed may have been forced to embark, on the destruction of its spiritual foundations, and that the much vaunted

classical approach to life would ultimately promote vanity, deceit, pride and spiritual alienation from the source of divine wisdom. Thus Michelangelo became a partisan of the Counter-Reformation and an unofficial collaborator of Tridentism; a venerable reactionary with a mounting distaste for empty modernity, fully aware that he was fighting a losing battle. In this unnerving struggle he laid bare his soul before his God as though at the apocalyptic Judgement. And all that is reprehensible and small is relegated to damnation; what has been purified and illuminated is raised up: thus it happens that neither angels nor liberated spirits are in need of wings; the falling and the rising are inherent. In brief, Michelangelo does not paint theology or eschatology dictated by set doctrines; he paints his own unconscious, expressing its nature and its workings by means of forms and symbols current in Christian thought. He sits in judgement upon himself and gives the world a demonstration of an artist's mystical phantasmagoria.

The centre is the God within, under the guise of Christ the Judge, though reminders of humanism have not been entirely discarded. For he seems an Apollo marked with the wound of Our Lord. The raised right hand of the naked Pantocrator draws up the blessed and banishes the damned. The left hand wards off, not the wicked in hell, but the wrathful martyrs. This and the emphatic gesture with which the enthroned and aureoled figure makes as if to rise convey the other-worldly vision of the artist. The wall recedes; infinity or the metacosmos opens out with the heavenly host streaming in, carrying the instruments of the Passion. The cross and the pillar at which Christ was scourged, saints, the Holy Virgin, seven angels trumpeting, the beatified, the risen dead, damned souls battling with angels, daemonic judges and the infernal henchmen Charon and Minos with their damned victims—the painting is a sea of bodies, full of significant movements; a truly astonishing vision.

It is impossible to picture accurately the initial impact of this titanic tribunal; the Pope prostrated himself before it in penitential

INTERIOR OF THE SISTINE CHAPEL

prayer. One may imagine it from a copy at Naples, carried out in 1540 by Marcello Venusti under the supervision of Michelangelo before the prudery of subsequent ages caused several figures, more naked than the Signorelli frescoes of Orvieto, to be painted over by Daniele da Volterra and others. (It also proves that a broad band of the original fresco has been sacrified to two doors and a wall incrustation. The pale blue of the interstices and the Virgin's cloak have suffered.) But these 'corrections' remained within careful bounds, although voices were periodically raised demanding the destruction of the whole. The reality brought home insistently by the great nudes continued to be misunderstood by religious zealots and hypocrites. And, as we shall see, Michelangelo left a sombre record of his quarrel with the pamphleteer, Pietro Aretino, who allied himself with his detractors. The 'Last Judgement' is carefully thought out and lucidly presented. With great mastery Michelangelo dispenses with the customary effects of geometrical construction, perspective and proportion, but draws the side walls into the over-all composition. Nevertheless, the main focal point is firmly placed in the central axis. The frescoes have darkened considerably since Michelangelo painted them, although he did keep the colours sparse and sombre, with browns, blues and greys predominating in an intentional contrast to the colourful, and often brilliant, ceiling frescoes. The colouring suits the solemnity of the theme. Not for nothing is the book containing the names of the blessed small, while that of the damned is enormous, as one can see from the group of apocalyptic angels beneath the Christ. So great a wave of terror passes through the massed figures of this Armageddon that even those admitted to Paradise seem fearful of their salvation. True to the two books, we see the resurrection from the dead on the lower right, with the Prophet who predicted the awakening of Israel (Ezekiel 37, 2-14) helping an old man to his feet; while to the left the eternally damned vanish into the maw of the devil,

The Last Judgement. Detail
Sistine Chapel

STUDY FOR THE LAST JUDGEMENT
MUSÉE BONNAT, BAYONNE

THE LAST JUDGEMENT. DETAIL
SISTINE CHAPEL

an allusion to Dante's *Inferno*. Here are the dreaded boatman
Charon, and Minos, Judge of the Underworld who, entwined by
snakes, is shown with an infernal grin and ass's ears—a caricature,
according to Vasari, of the Pope's Master of Ceremonies, Biagio
da Cesena, who during a visit to the Sistine Chapel had called the
whole thing a '*stufa d'ignudi*', a public bath full of nudities. Later
he complained to the Pope about his posting to hell. Paul III

THE LAST JUDGEMENT. DETAIL
SISTINE CHAPEL

refused to intervene, replying with true Tuscan wit that he had power over heaven and purgatory, but had no say at all in hell.

Another equally strange figure is found in heaven where we can see the gigantic naked Bartholomew among the saints demonstrating their instruments of torture. We recognize a hardly accidental likeness to Aretino, known from Titian's portrait. Aretino eventually attacked Michelangelo in one of his open letters—these were

PORTRAIT OF VITTORIA COLONNA
BRITISH MUSEUM

THE LAST JUDGEMENT. DETAIL
SISTINE CHAPEL

usually written after an attempt at extortion had failed—saying that the 'Last Judgement' showed less respect and decorum than his own salacious dialogues with courtesans. However that may be, in the folds of the flayed skin held by Bartholomew-Aretino we can see a likeness of Michelangelo. Did the artist intend to imply that he had flayed Aretino, or the other way round? The victim is Michelangelo himself, as we can deduce from his painful grimace. The robust Bartholomew-Aretino may be admitted to Paradise, while the artist sees himself as a caricature on a dead man's skin! One thing is striking; namely, the rebellious expression and the rolling

THE LAST JUDGEMENT.   DETAIL.   (SELF-PORTRAIT?)
SISTINE CHAPEL

eyes of the celestial company surrounding the Christ: that of Saint Peter on the right of Our Lord, holding the keys of the Kingdom, and of his counterpart on the left in whom Vasari saw Adam, also those of Saint Bartholomew and Saint Lawrence with the grid-iron, at the feet of Christ.   What does their attitude and expression imply? Not theological concepts, but an unresolved conflict in the artist's mind.   He sees no solution to the problem of evil, and therefore no true deliverance of mankind in the apocalyptic event. Michelangelo had not yet arrived at the great affirmation. The bliss of pure being that ranges far beyond the purgatory of morals, the 'felix culpa', had not yet been realized.

In spite of this implicit doubt, the total value of the fresco is incalculable and its psychological content inexhaustible. To compare it with earlier paintings of the Last Judgement or with Michelangelo's own premiminary sketches, is pointless. This fresco is and remains unique and ever new. No previous work can measure up to it; not even the physical strength and vigour of the Signorelli frescoes in the Cappella Brizio at the Duomo of Orvieto. Posterity continues to draw on the stupendous wealth of Michelangelo's *danse macabre*. But now the master had exhausted the potential of an art whose means and methods had proved inadequate to reveal the mystery of the identity of the human and the divine. It was necessary for him to surpass even himself. That he did do so is borne out by his late sculptures and architectural works. They are of this world in appearance only. The change is indicated by a dark female figure at the extreme left of the gigantic fresco, above the group of the risen dead. Impelled upwards as by longing, she lifts a face with half-closed eyes illuminated by a ray of grace, and her adoring hands holding an invisible cup, express the ineffable. She is not beautiful. She is wonderful in the proper sense of the word—full of wonder. The wrathful martyrs may rest on their sufferings and good works, but she personifies the purest faith.

MICHELANGELO ABANDONS FORMS THAT SHACKLE

Michelangelo had been among the initiators of the Renaissance, Mannerism and Baroque, but he remained medieval Man, and in his seventies shed his humanist gown and cloaked himself in Christian humility and heavenly dignity. One might compare this step to the metamorphosis of Thomas à Becket from Chancellor to Archbishop, saint and martyr. The change was indicated by Michelangelo's name. The tender genius of Ariosto senses this when he addresses the master, *'Michel, più che mortale, angiol divino'* ('Michael, more than mortal, angel of God'). From now on faith attained through love as his only hope and as the true meaning of his life and art came to Michelangelo through Vittoria Colonna, and remained with him. Theirs was a love in the best medieval tradition, familiar from the poetry of the Troubadours and Minnesänger, and from the bond between Dante and Beatrice, Laura and Petrarch. Some present-day attitudes might suggest that such a relationship be labelled 'patholo- gical', but Goethe in his *Faust* shows himself still aware of the psycho- logical and metaphysical implications of sublimated Eros. It is evident that, with a visual artist like Michelangelo, a love of this sort immediately became a sublime reality, more real and palpable than in the case of Dante or Petrarch, who had no sooner beheld their ideal than it was transposed into the figurative and spiritual domain. For Michelangelo his lady became an actual presence; for years she was accessible to his sight and hearing, though he never touched her. When she died, consumed by the ascetic in her, after more than ten years of mystical friendship, he, too, died to the world and filled the vacuum she had left with the symbols and poetic images of his inner vision. But in spite of his longing for death he remained confined to this vacuum and wrote: *'la morte è'l fin d'una prigione oscura'* ('Death is the end of a dark prison'). A total banishment of the artist's wish-dream of enchanting, sensual beauty followed. His gorgeous colouring was abandoned in the 'Last Judgement'. The entire sensual pagan 'Venusberg' disappeared from his works. The impact of Vittoria Colonna's faith and her noble, cultured mind helped to transform Michelangelo into a great religious artist.

Vittoria Colonna was born in 1492. Her father, Fabrizio Colonna, and her mother Agnese da Montefeltro, affianced her as a small child to the Marchese of Pescara who died while commanding at the battle of Pavia. Vittoria was not beautiful, and, perhaps because of this and her extreme modesty, he had not loved her. The widow retired to her castle at Ischia and did not marry again in spite of numerous suitors, attracted by her poet's fame, her wealth and her noble birth. She mourned deeply for her brilliant, but by no means faithful husband, and found solace only by turning her mind to God and

BUST OF BRUTUS. DETAIL. *c.* 1542
BARGELLO, FLORENCE

things divine. Hers was no sudden conversion. Highly intellectual, combining a charming if reserved manner with the humanist masculinity of the Renaissance *virago*, she was assailed by doubt, in spite of her deeply religious nature. At that time an enthusiastic group of dissidents from Catholic orthodoxy had gathered in Naples; among them the Spaniard Juan de Valdès, who had Protestant leanings, and the spectacular Capucine preacher Fra Bernardino Occhino, who later joined Calvin in Geneva. Vittoria listened to their doctrines. The heretical teachings of Luther and Calvin, with their new interpretation of the ideas of Saint Augustine, following upon the religious indifference of the late Renaissance, resulted in a religious revival after the Sack of Rome. When Vittoria Colonna moved to Rome, and in the summer, to Viterbo, a circle of remarkable men gathered round her. They were deeply preoccupied with religious questions, tending towards an extreme Augustinian doctrine and, without wishing to leave the Church, they shared Luther's conviction that faith alone—*sola fides*—and not works could affect salvation; an extremely unpredictable and unknowable salvation according to Calvin.

Had these aspiring souls lost sight of the Pauline postulate that faith without love or charity was useless? It is in the nature of love to do good works. The minimizing of works and the ensuing limitation of man's freedom in a deterministic doctrine of grace could only result in a heavy and gloomy conception of faith and charity. In a letter to Michelangelo Vittoria expresses her strange beliefs and speaks in terms that an implacable father confessor or a stern mother might use:

> My most excellent messer Michelangelo:
> So great is the fame which your ability confers, that you probably never have believed that time or anything else could bring it to an end. But since then the divine Light has entered your heart, showing you that earthly fame, however long-lived, suffers a second death. If, therefore, in your works you behold the goodness of Him who has made you a unique master, you may then realize that in my almost lifeless writings I merely thank the Lord that while writing them I offended Him less than I do in my leisure. I therefore beg you to accept this my will as a pledge for future works.
>
> Your obedient servant,
The Marchesa of Pescara

Like all that came from her, Michelangelo accepted as a precious gift this ardent and restrained letter, which told him nothing save that works would not count in paradise; he could see no fault in her. But she could not rob him of his belief in the necessity of works. It is attested by the statue of Leah for the final version of the mausoleum of Julius II, finished at that time. She is an emblem of active charity, and he has given her a laurel wreath to carry.

When Vittoria Colonna's friends, Michelangelo among them, met in the small church of San Silvestro al Quirinale, they discussed these religious and artistic matters. The Portuguese miniature-painter Francisco d'Ollanda describes their sessions in his four dialogues on painting. Michelangelo's poems tell, in his terse and expressive style, of the joys, preoccupations and torments that moved him and this group. It was at its most expressive when he addressed Vittoria, though much was left unsaid between the two ageing friends who cared for each other with a love made more perfect, by their renunciation, than that of lovers caught like netted birds in the mesh of earthly passion. Michelangelo's poems to Vittoria and the drawings he made for her, his frescoes in the Cappella Paolina, and the self-abnegation he shows in the mausoleum of Julius II by discarding his handsome slaves—all these testify to his deep feeling for her. It seems that after her death their dialogue continued more fervently, in greater solitude, finding expression in august architectural projects and in the last great 'Deposition from the Cross'.

The bust of Brutus, completed probably after the 'Last Judgement', was the sculptor's last proud relapse. He, who hated tyrants and yet was unable really to hate the Medici, and in the end could only love, made a rapid sketch for this bust and handed it to his pupil Calcagni; it was never finished. Mindful of Dante's Brutus placed between the jaws of Satan in an icy hell, Michelangelo did not warm to his subject. The Brutus had been commissioned by Florentine emigrants when the notorious Alessandro de' Medici was murdered by his kinsman Lorenzino. This deed was exalted by the republican Florentines, but it bore little resemblance to the dire judgement on the great Caesar.

Resignedly, Michelangelo at length finished the tomb of Pope Julius, which ended by being a setting for the 'Moses'. The extended deadline had once again been overstepped, but a Papal brief had relieved Michelangelo of all his obligations to the della Rovere heirs as long as he was engaged in painting the 'Last Judgement'. No sooner was this finished than Paul III ordered a series of frescoes for the

Conversion of Saint Paul. 1542-5
Cappella Paolina, Vatican

Cappella Paolina.   Duke Guidobaldo Rovere of Urbino was willing to content himself with the 'Moses' and two 'Slaves' by Michelangelo, in addition to three statues by Raffaello da Montelupo.   As the two 'Slaves' were nearly ready, nothing could have been easier; but now Michelangelo would not agree to this.   Instead, the obstinate old man proposed two statues, by his pupils, of Rachel and Leah as emblems of the active and the contemplative life, in reference to passages of Dante's *Purgatory* (*Purgatorio* XXVII, 94; XXVIII, 37; XXXIII, 119)[2], although these were not mentioned in the contract. His decision was no doubt due to the religious change in him wrought by Vittoria Colonna's influence.   He had no further use for mere sensual beauty.   It is nevertheless remarkable that Leah, as Active Charity, is treated as a figure of equal importance to Rachel, who stands for Faith.   Michelangelo proved himself a true son of the Church in turning a deaf ear to the new doctrine of faith alone, for in a faith supported by active charity divine grace is implicit.   As it is written in the Apostolic letter: 'Even so faith, if it has not works, is dead, being alone' (James 2,17).

The final version of the Papal mausoleum reflects the dichotomy in Michelangelo's being: it is both stirring and disappointing.   Even in its present form, including the earlier, richly ornamented lower storey and the austere upper storey with the reversed pilaster-obelisks, it bears the stamp of his planning and of his personality. The two complementary figures on either side of the 'Chosen of God', which in the end Michelangelo finished himself, give an impression of asymmetry and do not harmonize; they might have been carved by different sculptors.

Rachel is depicted in a Baroque posture, like a nun about to kneel, her head raised to heaven and her shoulders covered by a long veil, while Leah is a frontal statue with a folded robe, belted below the breasts and falling down to her naked feet; with her right hand she adjusts a headdress and coiled tresses while the left holds a laurel wreath instead of the crown of blossoms Dante gave her.   The head is turned slightly toward the left side of the tomb.   Compared to the 'Moses', these two statues are infinitely still and incorporeal; and yet each has a different kind of stillness.   Rachel is contemplating God with an intensity of adoration, but Leah stands quietly musing, like a personification of some heavenly blessing, yet reminiscent of the goddesses of ancient Greece. The draperies are treated in a way that differs basically from the 'wet garment' style. It is in the medieval tradition, giving relatively little emphasis to the body beneath the folds of the material. The symmetrical arrangement of the two silhouettes is achieved by giving the sides facing the 'Moses' uneven surfaces, and the sides averted from him reposeful, smoothly flowing lines, similar to those found on the Madonna Medici. Leah seems larger and more substantial than does Rachel in her half-kneeling posture.

On the south-east side of the Sistine Chapel and divided from it by the Sala Regia, Pope Paul III had built for him the Cappella Paolina as his private chapel, to use instead of the small, handsome shrine of Nicholas V in the upper storey of a Vatican tower. Here Michelangelo spent nearly ten years painting two frescoes. These were to be his last paintings, finished in his seventy-fifth year. The sacramental chapel which bore the Pope's name suggested the theme of Saint Paul's journey to Damascus when he heard the voice: 'Saul, Saul, why persecutest thou me?' Turning his back on his past, Saul became Paul, the Apostle to be, and in his rendering of this scene Michelangelo, too, turned from his past. His design for the chapel included an equally momentous scene from the life of Saint Peter for the opposite wall; he did not forget that the Church celebrates the feast of the two saints and martyrs of Rome on the same day, 29th June. In the first edition of his *Lives of the Painters* dated 1550, Vasari recounts that Michelangelo had painted the 'Handing of the Keys to Saint Peter' opposite the 'Conversion of Saint Paul'. In the second edition of 1567 he rectifies this assertion and speaks of a 'Crucifixion of Saint Peter'. What had happened? Had Vasari made a mistake in the first place? The episodes of the journey to Damascus and of the handing of the keys are the most momentous in the lives of the Apostles and have always been of vital importance to the Church of Rome. It could be that their logical sequence was changed by Michelangelo under the impact of this personal experience during

that period, for to express this brought some relief to his despairing heart. Everything that Michelangelo wrought was a personal record, a journal in which the various themes and their treatment are more or less open confessions. The tragic blow which fell while he was hard at work in the Paolina and broke his heart was the death of Vittoria in February 1547, the year in which he also lost Sebastiano del Piombo, the only pupil who had understood him. Could these events have led him to replace the scene of triumph with a scene of gruesome martyrdom? From early youth, Michelangelo had lived with the awareness of death, and in old age he remembered it through constant meditations on the Cross and the spectacle of the Crucifixion. From the cross to which he has been fastened upside down, Saint Peter—perhaps representing Michelangelo—turns a terrible gaze towards those who look at him from the outside: the credulous, and those who give lip service only, the art enthusiasts and the merely curious; masters and slaves, but all of them part and parcel of a weak and fallible humanity.

The two frescoes—little known, because not accessible to the general public—fill even the admirers of the master's work with dismay. They seem harsh and lacking in depth and perspective, cold and desolate, and that in spite of the sketchily marked landscape and a multitude of figures. But a close examination shows that, compared to that of the 'Last Judgement' the colouring has once more become rich and sensuous. It reminds us faintly of Masaccio, but is fortunately less monotonous. The protagonists of these frescoes, where grace and beauty are no longer found, seem to be possessed by a frenzy both holy and unholy. It is evident that Raphael's best frescoes from the Stanze inspired the colour and the composition.

When the frescoes of the Paolina were cleaned in the nineteen-thirties, it was found that they had suffered very badly, in parts as badly as Leonardo's 'Last Supper' in Milan. Later, the patches and faded places were restored, resulting in the hard and glossy smoothness we see today, which has replaced the glorious finish and composi-

CONVERSION OF SAINT PAUL. DETAIL

tion of the original. (Photographs taken in 1933 give some idea of what the freshly cleaned frescoes looked like, and one can but marvel at the audacity of restorers willing to compete with the geniuses of this world.) As they stand, the frescoes are still of the greatest interest. In them Michelangelo had acquired a new subtlety of drawing not previously achieved by this master of the linear. The composition shows great depth of feeling obtained by the use of chiaroscuro, the contrasting use of light and darkness that foreshadows Rembrandt and testifies to the heroic virtuosity of the aged master. A focal line traverses the 'Conversion of Saint Paul'; its progression at once reveals the meaning of the composition. Starting at the top left it flows diagonally, along the figure of Christ descending and a beam of light. It follows a figure with raised fingers and another, bent over the fallen Saul, and circumscribes the ellipse of this body. From his right leg it curves back and upward in the direction of a horse galloping in the background, and loses itself in the undulating contours of the mountains with a vision of the heavenly Jerusalem faintly outlined in their folds—unless we accept a more literal explanation and call it Damascus. Note that this line has the shape of a bishop's staff and sums up the whole incident in symbolic form: Saul is destined to be shepherd and overseer of the people. The term 'bishop' means overseer. The high-light on the head of Saul and on the horse's head confirms the symbolic meaning; the dim awareness of fallen man is touched by the lightning flash of grace, and as universal consciousness awakens in him, he loses his animal torpor and gains true knowledge. Saul is not shown as a young soldier but as a bearded old man; perhaps an allusion to the octogenarian Pope Paul. The Acts of the Apostles make no mention of a horse, but this version of the event, which was copied by many later painters, is pregnant with meaning and a host of earthly and heavenly spectators indicate various degrees of participation. These witnesses, too, are absent from the Acts.

In the 'Crucifixion of Saint Peter', everything is centred in the fearful event; in triumph over pain and suffering. Solace comes from the spectacle of fortitude, confidence and will-power; the intrepid character of Saint Peter. As in the fresco of Saint Paul, the main prota-

CRUCIFIXION OF SAINT PETER. 1546-50
CAPPELLA PAOLINA, VATICAN

gonist fits into an ellipse placed in the centre of the cross, extended on
four sides by the disposition of the figures. This device lends to the
design a clarity and strength which is absent from the restless Damascus

scene, because there the fallen Saul appears suspended in mid-air at the lower edge of the picture, and the accompanying figures occupy different levels of space. In the 'Crucifixion', on the other hand, most of the figures are vertical; only those near the centre give the impression of rotating round the martyr. Their features betray the utmost horror, especially those of the women on the lower right who tremble with terror, and several onlookers seem on the verge of madness.

During the last fifteen years of his life, Michelangelo did not touch a brush. His architectural works and attempts at sculpture were sermons delivered in the guise of three-dimensional art.

THE ARCHITECT: FLIGHT FROM THE TEMPORAL INTO THE ETERNAL

Apart from a few minor commissions, none of Michelangelo's buildings were finished in his lifetime. He was destined to see them with his mind's eye only, as Moses had seen the Promised Land; as the deaf Beethoven heard his melodies with an inner ear. In this respect Michelangelo resembled the medieval master-builders, whose venerable ranks he closed as the architect of the central edifice and dome of Saint Peter's. Indeed, the Basilica of the Vatican is the last great Christian cathedral, early Baroque or Mannerist—or rather, Michelangelesque—in style, but still having basic affinities with the methods of the medieval masons' guilds,

In 1546, after the completion of the 'Conversion of Saint Paul' the Pope entrusted Michelangelo with his great Roman projects: the Capitol, Saint Peter's and the Palazzo Farnese. Preoccupation with architectural plans is, therefore, discernible in the 'Crucifixion of Saint Peter'. In 1547 the ageing Pope nominated him prefect of the works at Saint Peter's, the earlier plans for which Michelangelo revised and simplified.

Michelangelo was not only a creator on a vast scale: he was a des-troyer. No longer satisfied with partial beauty, nor with the artist's ideal of beauty manifest in a multiplicity of forms (which so easily degenerates into mere good taste and aestheticism), he aspired to the

PALAZZO FARNESE, ROME

beauty of the One, Infinite and Eternal. It was inevitable that his
architectural detail should become less functional and tectonic, and
should be used as a signature and symbol, or as a catalyst to heighten
the significance of a whole that was no longer of this world. All
the details—windows, tympana, consoles, doors, cornices, columns,
pilasters and so on were so placed as to add strength to the over-all
impression, and totally deprived of the independence they had
enjoyed in the gay and self-confident Renaissance, when each part in
its perfection became a means to an end, as for instance the cornice
of the Palazzo Farnese, or the capitals of the Palazzo dei Conservatori
on the Capitol. Now Michelangelo was concerned solely with

worshipping the highest God, and even his secular buildings acquired a devotional flavour.

With this aim in mind he pulled and massed the parts together more boldly than any of his forerunners had done, subordinating them to the great Unity. Now more than ever he saw it as spirit incarnate in form, but not, as before, a complex series of forms; rather as a single, indivisible body which the demands of inward symmetry and artistic integrity lend a triple nature; which becomes, in fact, a Trinity. Architecture offered him the most immediate opportunity to express this.

Antonio da Sangallo the Younger died in 1546, and the bulk of his unfinished work fell to Michelangelo. How '*il terribile*' grappled with his task is evident from the palace which Cardinal Alessandro Farnese had long ago ordered Sangallo to build. Elected to the Papacy, Alessandro announced a contest for the cornice design, which Michelangelo won; whereupon he was left to finish the building. The master changed the character of the edifice completely by adding an impressive cornice with Farnese lilies and a superstructure to the uppermost storey, and by emphasizing the centre storey with a noble window and balcony, surmounted by the family escutcheon. Two more crests on either side are a later addition. An excellent drawing of 1840 by the architect of the Louvre, Hector Martin Lefuel, shows the façade as it was before it was spoilt by additions to the central axis.

The vertical edges of the building were reinforced by rustic work. The windows of the upper storey, with Romanesque arches surmounted by detached triangular cornices, lend an air of organic growth and lightness to the otherwise massive and portentous palace. One is reminded of the 'growing castle' in Strindberg's *Dream Play*; and where Sangallo had wavered between a unity composed of many harmonious elements, and a single, dominant theme, Michelangelo brought everything under a common denominator. The airy, charming arcades of the courtyard were surmounted by stern walls with angulate pilasters and exceptionally beautiful windows with detached cornices.

Every façade is, of course, a mirror or a mask. Michelangelo was

very fond of masks and we find them often in his works. Did he intend them as a kind of signature? Did their suggestion of personal anonymity appeal to him? Or was it his intention to brand everything as false, illusory; to declare that 'All is vanity'? One thing is certain: these masks impose silence. Not in vain did he retire ultimately into the abstractions of architecture, and it is immaterial whether the impetus to do so came from without or from his own soul.

STUDY FOR THE VESTIBULE OF THE BIBLIOTECA LAURENZIANA,
FLORENCE

The sumptuous cornice of the Palazzo Farnese, which replaces the *'ignobile tetto'*, is an unusual feature of the master's work. Was it inspired by the pride of the patrician, or by that of the artist and genius? Vittoria addressed him as *'mio unico maestro'*, *'mio singolarissimo amico'* or *'magnifico messer'*. Cardinal Ippolito Medici presented him with a fine Turkish steed complete with groom and we may assume that, mounted like a great noble, he visited the Marchesa of Pescara, Cardinals, friends, and humanists of every sort. He loved to ride in the countryside of the Campagna, to visit its silent monasteries and sometimes dreamed of retiring to the hills of Latium. In all this he modelled himself upon Vittoria Colonna, admiring her pride, her devotion, and her love of art and learning. She was his Madonna, present and yet wholly unattainable; an image of the heavenly and earthly mother. The key to his emotional and sex life is to be found in his relationship to the mother figure, which partly explains his addiction to young boys and *epheboi*. But always he remained essentially lonely, isolated by the quality of his genius and, like many a great artist, he was to a certain extent androgynous.

Unique among Michelangelo's achievements was the architectural conquest of the Capitoline hill, that is to say, the depression between the ancient temple of Juno Moneta—who had survived as the Madonna of Aracoeli—and that of Jupiter Capitolinus. This was indeed the heart of the Roman Imperium.

In his earlier great works Michelangelo had repeatedly expressed himself in cosmogonic allusions and metaphors. On the Capitol he devised a complete plan of Creation, attested by the strange floor mosaics of the Capitol, laid in 1940 after etchings made from his long-forgotten designs. On the top of the sacred hill the master created in effect a model of the timeless, spaceless ideal universe. The three palaces demonstrate the mystery of divine Revelation. The magnificent downward sweep of the double staircase with its platform and its statues of river-gods symbolizes the divine descent from Truth into Goodness and Beauty, in other words, into Light and the Word, indicated by the polarity of the two lateral palaces which flank the square at a slightly diagonal angle.

The master's project was accepted but subsequently modified in places. The central Palazzo del Senatore was begun in 1546. Michelangelo is responsible for the outside staircase only, and in 1588 a new bell tower was added. The Palazzo dei Conservatori was completed in 1568 by Prospero Bocca Paduli and Tommaso Cavalieri. Giacomo del Duca enlarged it later and transformed the central window into a balcony. The Museo Capitolino lying to the left, close to Aracoeli, was built 1644-55, under Innocent X. Michelangelo lived to supervise the building of the Palazzo dei Conservatori, but the changes wrought in the original project by his successors were not to its advantage. Giacomo del Duca had destroyed the hieratic concord of seven porticoes with pillars, surmounted by seven windows ranged like archangels. And it was a mistake to smother the sides of the Cordonata, the gently rising staircase of the Capitol, with all kinds of plants. Everything should have been carried out in stone, as if to exclude whim and fancy from a cosmic conception: for this is the acropolis of the present millennium, the fruit of a unique individual mind.

The visitor from the North is inevitably struck by the noble balustrades of the three palaces. There are no visible roofs. As we have seen, these were regarded as an impure architectural form. A sloping line would, it was felt, have destroyed the balance between vertical and horizontal planes. Gently slanting lines were confined to vertical planes and used symmetrically. The Renaissance abhorred steep Gothic gables and towers. In spite of its Ionic and Corinthian capitals the Palazzo dei Conservatori and its counterpart remind us of a Doric temple. The broadly spaced ground plan is the same, and so is the effect it gives of striving upwards from mother earth. One is tempted to imagine that Michelangelo might have come across some belated discovery of ancient architecture and recreated it in travertine, the Roman limestone similar to the poros of classical antiquity.

The structure of the Palazzo dei Conservatori is an astonishing demonstration of the laws of the universe. This is the real reason for the inherent strength and character of the building which, like every great feat of architecture, cannot be explained solely in technical and aesthetic terms. The oppressive atmosphere, the unfathomable gloom of the lower storey, planned as a hall with seven square openings that seem like portals to the underworld, flanked by columns that confine the huge supporting pillars: all this indicates the necessary existence of darkness, evil, and negative power more eloquently than a host of theological or philosophical speculation. The building seems an illustration of a saying by Rabbi Israel ben Eliezer, founder of Hasidism (who lived two hundred years after Michelangelo): 'Evil

HEAD OF A SATYR
BRITISH MUSEUM

is the seat of Goodness'; and, correspondingly, the void of the lower
storey broods above the barren, stony soil.   The small columns with
rich Ionic capitals support massive mouldings and the beautiful
window zone.   They are reinforced by strong pilasters with Corinthian capitals resting on plinths which carry the architrave with
cornices and balustrades reminiscent of the 'spirit moving above the
face of the waters'   The splendid concord of the windows, with
cornices carved with shell patterns, suggests the harmony of the

realm of souls, for every soul is a window on to the world. The total effect is obtained by an indescribable visual brilliance of proportion and counterpoint. How Michelangelo came to conceive these plans we do not know; enough that this incomparable metaphor of a universal order took shape in his mind and became an architectural masterpiece.

Michelangelo set the seal on this plan by removing the equestrian statue of Marcus Aurelius, which the Romans had long believed to be Constantine the Great, from the Lateran, and placing it on a pedestal of his design in the centre of the Capitoline piazza. As emblem of the Imperial power of Rome, the Caesar holding sway over a limitless area rises from the centre of the sun, whose twelve rays branch out into a linear pattern of multiple dimensions; by means of intersecting lines six times twelve concentric fields are obtained. It is clear that in conjunction with the twelve-pointed sun upon which he rides, they represent the planets (which designation includes sun and moon), passing through the twelve mansions of the Zodiac. As an assiduous reader of the *Divine Comedy* Michelangelo may have come by these ideas, familiar to other medieval minds, Dürer among them. The monarchic idea, too, derives from Dante. The whole design fits into an ellipse which represents the earthly correspondence to the divine sphere, but it is an oval which contains two focal points because dualism in the world had displaced the true centre. It is no accident or artist's whim that the number seven is the key theme of the Capitol. It is found in the mystical speculation of all ages, reaching from remote antiquity through Jakob Böhme to modern times.

All extant documents and the results of modern research attest that the Old Basilica of Saint Peter's was a beautiful church and the joy of every pilgrim. But it was falling to pieces, and the prevalent taste for the spectacular determined the Popes to pull down the venerable building and replace it by a new and more imposing church. Many plans were advanced and discarded; many changes made. Each Pope and each newly appointed architect criticized, chopped and changed the earlier plans. What emerged were bits and fragments,

THE PORTA PIA. PARTIALLY DESIGNED BY MICHELANGELO, ROME

the most excellent being those left by Bramante, though artists like
Raphael, Baldassare Peruzzi and Antonio da Sangallo the Younger
had made their contributions. Weighty tomes were compiled recording the complicated history of this building. In 1547 Pope Paul III
entrusted Michelangelo with the supervision of the plans, but years
went by before he managed to introduce some order into them and

impose unity on the inchoate mass of designs and materials. He reduced Bramante's elaborate plans to a central edifice and a mighty dome. This dome, finished after his death, became the largest in the world. The central aisle has been spoilt by a nave and a façade whose cold secularity is redeemed solely by Bernini's magnificent colonnades. One must see Michelangelo's Saint Peter's from the west side to appreciate what was intended here; likewise one should cross the nave and, disregarding the bronze canopy and all later Baroque additions, look at the cruciform transepts and up towards the vaulted cupola.

Bramante had envisaged a square dome with four towers and a light, balanced arrangement of aisles and cloisters, the whole made up of autonomous and coordinated parts. Michelangelo's plan was grander and more simple, with an elliptical parabolic cupola dominating the whole design. Today its gigantic silvery shape against the Roman sky recalls the Orphic egg of the Greek myth floating in Aither, the primordial aether. The internal structure of the church is cruciform, with barrel vaulting in Bramante's manner, while the castle-like façade suggests worldly rather than spiritual dominion. The gallery at the base of the cupola is almost Gothic in character. The walls below, broken by superimposed windows in groups of two and three, wedged between steeply rising pilasters with angulate Corinthian capitals, support the architrave, the cornice and the powerful attic storey. All this is but a basis for, and a prelude to, the great dome which dominates and blesses the Campagna Romana, or what is left of it today.

In architecture, detail is everything: the curves and outlines of the almost rhomboid cupola surpass all other silhouettes of its kind, even that of Brunelleschi's cupola for the Duomo in Florence and those of the great mosques of Istanbul and Cairo. If one views the dome of Saint Peter's from the south or west, whence the weaknesses of later architects are not apparent, its impact, the testament of the aged Michelangelo, makes one wonder what the secret of this dome can be. Theoretically, it should not have been difficult to design. In fact only one man was capable of devising it, and granted the inspiration to carry it out. In harmonizing elements which are eternally and fundamentally opposed, his genius drew upon the accumulated wisdom of his life. The pointed cupola reveals the mystery of the universe; the miracle of reconciliation between God and man. Shining above the Eternal City, the silver-grey dome radiates love.

In his eighty-fifth year or thereabouts, Michelangelo ordered a large wooden model of the dome. It has been preserved, and proves that his successors kept more or less closely to the original. Deviations are confined mainly to three particulars: instead of confining themselves to the proposed self-contained triangular window cornices, they alternate them with segment cornices. Between the ribs of the vaulting run three concentric and ascending groins to each section, breaking and enlivening the bare, vaulted surfaces. The handsome consoles of the attic above the tambour have been omitted. When one looks at the building the feeling persists that something is missing here, for the bare right angles are abrupt and unmotivated. Why were the consoles left out? Probably because of the prevalent aversion to the Gothic style; any suggestion of the buttress was to be avoided, although in this particular instance it was needed and is in fact present, though camouflaged by Neoclassical pillars in pairs. Here more than in any of his other works the medievalist tastes of the aged Michelangelo, still so fertile of mind, shine through the 'draperies' of antiquity. Saint Peter's is a medieval dream; in its every rhythm it aspires to heaven and glorifies God. The cupola is the apotheosis of the Romanesque and the Gothic arch, with a lantern that in spite of its classical columns and candelabra reminds us of a belfry studded with mysterious carvings. This archetype of a Baroque church is made of the stuff of Gothic cathedrals and is the ultimate perfection of Brunelleschi's pointed cupola. Saint Peter's is a last great psalm in stone, intoned by a belated Gothic mystic, at a time when Christian thought was about to succumb to the manic compulsion of rational doubt and scientific superstitions.

Traces of Michelangelo's architectural activities are found in other parts of Rome. There are, for example, the sombre, crenellated bastions of the Porta Pia, where it is evident that the architect was primarily a sculptor. The central section, belonging to the

MODEL FOR THE DOME OF SAINT PETER'S, ROME

19th century, greatly weakens the dignified appearance of the original. The master built the Carthusian cloisters and the somewhat clumsy church of Santa Maria degli Angeli into the original structure of the Thermae of Diocletian. The sanctuary of San Giovanni dei Fiorentini and the outside staircase of the 'Nicchione' of the Belvedere, at the Giardino della Pigna, should also be mentioned. Here, and in several other instances, Michelangelo's plans were altered and disfigured by his collaborators and successors. It is also believed that the bridge of the Santa Trinità in Florence, blown up in the second world war but since restored, is to be attributed to a drawing by him. The effect of his style on his time is incalculable, and perhaps no other single artist has had such a far-reaching influence. He is the father of the last group of European architects to deserve that name; men who kept alive a tradition of building until the moment when utilitarian engineering took over. We must, however, make one reservation; namely that Michelangelo's countless imitators did not grasp his spiritual significance. They weakened his style by interpreting it according to their lights.

MICHELANGELO THE POET

To speak of Michelangelo's poems means to speak of his torment and subsequent purging through his Platonic love for Vittoria Colonna. In her he saw celestial beauty beside which all other beauty was as dust. It was only after entering the sphere of her rare personality that he became a true poet. Until then his verse had merely been an imaginative escape from cares and sorrows and the pangs of an oversensitive conscience. It is questionable whether he found poetry as much of a relief as did Goethe, who maintained that to give poetic expression to his emotional problems generally solved them.

Michelangelo's poetry is like the cry of a man subjected to torture. His verse more or less corresponds to the sketches and preliminary studies for his works, which meant less to him than they did to most other artists. He seldom kept to these designs or to the preliminary contours traced in the wet lime wash of his frescoes. From Goethe's innumerable notes, plans, letters and fragments of conversation it would be possible to reconstruct almost his entire life's work, but not much can be gleaned from Michelangelo's poems and essays. His sketches and poems were savage outbursts; '*sfoghi*', as the Italians call that sort of thing, the allergic reactions of his temper to the irritant of his surroundings.

The poems read like the lament of a man who witnessed the disruption of the universal order set out in the *Divine Comedy;* a man longing to re-establish the harmony of the medieval world but unable to do so, and knowing it merely as the unhappy sense of something lacking. The key to this torment is given when he exclaims:

> *Vorrei voler, Signor, quel ch'io non voglio,*
> *Tra 'l foco e 'l cor di ghiaccio un vel asconde,*
> *Che 'l foco ammerza; onde non corrisponde*
> *La penna all'opra, e fa bugiardo 'l foglio...*

(I would will, my Lord, what I do not will.
Between the fire and the ice-cold heart a veil is interposed,
which the fire absorbs; meanwhile what I write
does not correspond to what I do, and makes a lie of this page...)[3]

But in the end he willed what he did not wish to do. In his last poems and sculptures he accepted the will of God and identified it with his own.

One imagines his great soul overshadowed by Eros-Thanatos, the mysterious twins of love and death; the transcendent love of the Eternal, and longing for the extinction of all that is imperfect and hardened into self-love. Giovanni Amendola called Michelangelo 'the most passionate lover of love in history'. He was consumed by love long before he met Tommaso Cavalieri whom he deemed the perfect man; and that divine envoy and 'earthly counterpart of the radiant angels', Vittoria Colonna. All his days he was a beggar at the feet of Eros, filled with the desire to be absolved in the infinite love of God. The actual appearance in his life of Vittoria Colonna decided him to embrace unconditional faith, resulting in a true humility, purged of the rebellion expressed in the *'Prigioni'* against the paradoxes of existence. All that was left was his thirst for God, cleansed of all artistic and worldy ambition. His love of God

BACK VIEW OF A WOMAN
LOUVRE, PARIS

became a longing for death; a secret trust in a perfection beyond, which was unattainable in this world.

Resolute abnegation is the subject of his late poems: *'Più l'alma acquista, più 'l mondo perde'* ('In measure as the soul gains the world loses') or *'l'arte e la morte non van ben insieme'* ('Art and death do not go together'). But in spite of his belief that this was necessary for the final liberation of the soul he could not bring himself to renounce his art completely. His compromises were the last, much more abstract and 'artless' groups of the Pietà, conceived as pure liturgy and prayer, and poems whose merits are spiritual rather than literary; the spontaneous outpourings of a pilgrim to eternity who has moved on to a zone between heaven and earth.

The conqueror of beauty who was also her servant does not seem to have been alive to the aesthetic possibilities of sound, nor did he hesitate to call a spade a spade or attempt, as all the great poets had done, to mitigate coarseness by poetic form. That is why some of his poems seem so modern. This applies to the angry and sarcastic epigrams in which he describes the filth around his house, or his physical discomfort while working on the scaffold in the Sistina.

In Italy, Michelangelo has sometimes been called an Etruscan Platonist. The clear light of Platonic consciousness emanates from him, but at the same time he is earthbound, like the chthonian Etruscans, the painters and sculptors of death, or of a simulated life beyond the grave. Michelangelo had the Etruscan passion, still surviving in his race, for his native soil; he bought land, he perpetually hankered after rural solitude, and when he went into exile, he talked of committing suicide.

Of course, he did not really intend to take his own life. He merely felt an overwhelming urge to cleanse himself of mortal taint. It was his sorrow that he could not be perfect, could not love God as he wished, and that by his inner complexity and contradictions he denied Him. The beatific concept of a heavenly Father was foreign to his nature. He, who admired the noble Etruscan hardness of Dante and wished to resemble him, felt deeply involved with mortality and with the Old Testament. The creator of the 'Moses' and the 'Elohim'

HEAD OF A SATYR
LOUVRE, PARIS

became increasingly aware of the divine command forbidding man to make a graven image and bow down to it precisely because, in spite of this genius, he was unable to do so. That is why towards the end, in the 'Pietà Rondanini' and the 'Pietà Palestrina', his art became so abstract. This final phase is described in his last poem; those well-nigh untranslatable verses, cryptic as a forgotten script, even in the original. In them his soul, burning among the graven images of stone, asks to be cleansed of all false imaginings.

The struggle and this grief are particularly apparent in two sonnets of his extreme of age. The first was written in 1550 and addressed to God:

Deh, fammiti vedere in ogni loco:
Se da mortal bellezza arder mi sento,
appresso al tuo mi sarà foco ispento,
e io nel tuo sarò, com'ero, in foco.

Signor mio caro, i'te solo chiamo e 'n voco
contro l'inutil mio cieco tormento;
tu sol può rinnovarmi fuora drento
le voglie, e 'l senno, e 'l valor lento ch'è sì poco:
Tu desti al tempo ancor quest'alma diva,
e 'n questa spoglia ancor fragiloe stanca
l'incarcerasti, e con fiero destino.

Che poss'io altro, che così non viva?
Ogni ben senza te, Signor, mi manca;
il cangiar sorte è sol poter divino.

(Oh make me see you in every place! If I feel aflame with mortal beauty, before your fire my flame will be spent, and I, as I have been, in yours will burn. My dear Lord, I call and invoke you alone against my fruitless, blind torment. You can only renew, inside and out, my wisdom, wishes and my little worth; you decreed this divine soul still shall live in time and be imprisoned in this tired and fragile husk, with a proud fate. How can I change and not go on

STUDY OF A SEATED WOMAN
MUSÉE CONDÉ, CHANTILLY

like this? Without you, Lord, every good is withheld from me; the
power divine alone can alter fate.)

Almost all of Michelangelo's verses are poems of love, addressed
to worthy and unworthy objects, but always speaking of the loss
of self in love; therefore, in God. The objects of his ardent love

are substitutes for divine beauty, truth and goodness. 'Death for the sake of beauty' is the *leitmotif* running through his entire poetry, which scales the greatest heights in sonnets written for Vittoria Colonna, and through the earthly form of the Madonna-image reaches the sublime.

> *Giunto è già 'l corso della vita mia*
> *Con tempestoso mar per fragil barca*
> *Al comun porto, ov'a render si varca*
> *Giusta ragion d'ogni opra trista e pia.*
>
> *Onde l'affettuosa fantasia,*
> *Che l'arte si fece idolo, e monarca,*
> *Conosco ben quant'era d'error carca*
> *E qual c'a mal suo grado ogn'uom desia.*
> *Gli amorosi pensier, già vani e lieti,*
> *Che fian'or, s'a due morti m'avvicino?*
> *D'una son certo, e l'altra mi minaccia.*
>
> *Nè pinger, nè scolpir fia più che queti*
> *L'anima volta a quell'Amor divino*
> *Ch'aperse a prender noi in croce le braccia.*

(The course of my life is set, through the tempestuous sea in a fragile boat, to the common port, where man crosses over to give account of every mean and pious deed. Where my fond fantasy, of making art an idol and a king, I now know well, was full of error, and that which every man desires to his own harm. The loving thoughts, which once were vain and slight, what help are they, now that I approach my double death? Of one I'm certain and the other menaces me. Painting or sculpture can no longer soothe the soul turned towards that Love divine which to possess us, opens wide its arms.)[4]

Thomas Mann has justly observed that Michelangelo never loved for the sake of being loved and in fact felt unworthy of it. In love, he was the anvil rather than the hammer. Only death brought him final illumination.

The drawings of Old Masters are either preliminary studies or sketches, *aide-mémoire*, designs, or the outlines for oils and frescoes. They are seldom an end in themselves. Neither the artist nor the layman valued the fragmentary and approximate, the preliminary and 'primitive' as, rightly or wrongly, we do today. The old masters were apt to conceal the preliminary stages of their work and often destroyed them, unless they were lost through carelessness and use. We therefore do not possess many of their attested drawings, with the exception of a few by artists like Dürer, Holbein and Rembrandt, who had strong leanings towards graphic art.

Apart from his studies for large projects, Michelangelo left few drawings; those that exist were made for the two people he loved most, Cavalieri and Vittoria Colonna, and were intended as symbols and tokens of love. We are, therefore, tempted to see in many of the drawings attributed to him the works of his pupils and imitators. Most reliably attested are the sketches of his old age. As for the remaining material, expert opinions differ widely. One would have thought that if these fragments were so unique and of a quality equal to the frescoes and sculptures, doubts as to their authenticity would not have arisen. Be that as it may, today we enjoy the powerful drawings attributed to Buonarroti without probing too deeply into the complex reasons for our pleasure.

The subject matter was limited: it would be even more so were there not, within this limitation, a universal human significance Thus there are no landscapes, no representations of dwellings, animals (except for dream creatures in the shape of horses, swans and eagles), no ornaments outside the architectural drawings. All we find are human heads and bodies; an anatomical world-theatre of limbs in movement, the symbols of a dynamic aspiration purged of all physiognomy. Every element of the picturesque, of frivolity and things

THE FALL OF PHAETON
BRITISH MUSEUM

temporal, including shadows, is partly or wholly eliminated. There is no room for complicated feats of technique; for the use of high-lights or coloured paper, all of which he abhorred. Everything is stated briefly and succinctly, the figures are hieroglyphs of passionate aspiration, absorbed in playing their part on the universal stage. Michelangelo's drawings constitute the most anthropomorphous art that ever was. The complete *œuvre*—including the doubtful pieces in the manner much admired by his awed contemporaries—

MADONNA AND CHILD WITH SAINT JOHN
LOUVRE, PARIS

are a clear record of his inner feelings and the stages of his development. They illustrate his progression, beginning with an uncompro-
mising and explicit statement of the natural world drawn in clear
outlines, groping his way through the world of dream and purgatory
towards a world of grace; delicate, restrained and full of light. After
an initial harshness, even ponderousness, his line became at first more
economical and simple to the point of sparseness, discarding all that
was non-essential. Towards the end, it dissolved in gentle planes,

ethereal cloud and the *sfumato* of a diaphanous atmosphere; it had become quite immaterial. With increasing spirituality, matter became a pure expression of metaphysical vision. In conformity with this development Michelangelo preferred pen drawing in his younger days, and later took to black and red chalk.

We need not praise Michelangelo's drawings unduly. However perfect they may be in detail, hardly one of them is wholly satisfying. To praise the waste products of his drawing board, the results of an excess of ideas and creative powers, and to place them on a par with the great works would be to minimize his genius.

It is almost impossible to date his drawings. Each critic and every scholar has come to different conclusions. But it is not essential to know their sequence. It is much more important to meditate on them and divine what they tell us of Michelangelo, the man. We must content ourselves with a few brief indications. Vasari says that the 'Fall of Phaeton', in black chalk (in the Royal Library, Windsor), is one one of the drawings presented by the sixty-year-old master to Tommaso Cavalieri. Under the guise of a Greek myth he depicts the Fall; his own and that of mankind. The composition is a step-pyramid of moving, interlocking bodies. At the summit, Zeus, mounted on an eagle, flings his thunderbolt at the youth who, incapable of controlling his four horses, veers off his solar course and plunges into the river Eridanus. Huddled together beside an unconcerned river-god are the Heliads, Phaeton's sisters and daughters of the Sun-god, and his friend Kyknos changed into a swan. In this instance the powerful foreshortenings and contortions, although they initiate the outward forms of Mannerism, are indispensable to the expression of a catastrophe. Michelangelo must have thought of the seventeenth Canto of the *Inferno*:

> *Maggior paura non credo che fosse,*
> *quando Fetòn abbandonò li freni*
> *per che'l ciel, come pare ancor, si cosse;*

(Not greater was the dread, when Phaeton the reins let drop at random, whence high heaven, whereof signs yet appear, was wrapt in flames.)[5]

The isolation in space of the three groups, which Michelangelo finished more carefully than any of this other drawings, is pregnant with meaning.

In an early pen drawing of the Madonna (in the Louvre) inspired by Leonardo, the sorrow of Saint Anne infuses the whole group with a sense of michelangelesque solitude. The Virgin defends her radiance and that of the Child, drawn in light *sfumato*, against the sombrenes of her own mother. Yet the technique of this drawing is still painstaking and complicated.

After these two difficult works, let us look at the study for 'Adam Expelled from Paradise' (in the Casa Buonarroti, Florence). It would be hard to find greater perfection of drawing in western art. It is drawn in the style of the Sistine Chapel subjects, with noble, clearly outlined contours. This drawing alone would be enough to show us the supreme and unequalled status of the master.

The expulsion of Adam from Paradise is paradigmatic of Michelangelo's being; of his type of sensibility and his work. The torment of sin, initially disregarded in pagan denial of bodily shame, and the resulting delight in the structure of human form fashioned in the image of God; this very torment gained an increasing hold over the artist, and is more evident in his drawings than anywhere else. There, pleasure changes to doubt and irony, and finally to a feeling akin to disgust and negation of the body, clothed from now on in a robe of suffering and penitence. This certainly did not arise from intellectual realization of the apparent senselessness and shame of human destiny, nor from gloomy philosophizing on the incomprehensibility of existence, but from a higher plane of awareness whose insight was expressed in forms addressed to the eye and to the touch. If one keeps this in mind one will understand the meaning of Michelangelo's drawings, and why for instance the Heliads and daughters of the Sun-god appear like witches. Perhaps under the influence of Leonardo da Vinci, who was his equal if not his superior, he searched for a formula to embody the androgynous divine man. Goethe in *Mignon,* the counterpart or opposite pole of *Wilhelm Meister,* and Balzac in *Séraphitus,* have attempted this, but something strange and almost repellent pertains to most androgynes; witness the ambiguous

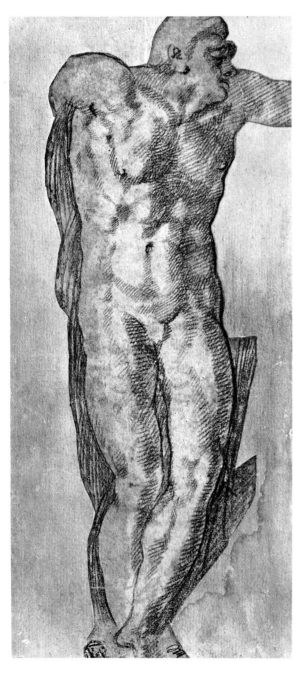

STUDY OF A NUDE MAN
LOUVRE, PARIS

images of Bacchus-Saint John the Baptist by Leonardo. The androgyne cannot really be portrayed in human terms; Plato therefore
visualized it as a sphere.

Yet Michelangelo's heroic heads, in drawings like the Sibyl (at
the Ashmolean) and another fine head at the Casa Buonarroti, have
an androgynous character. In both cases the sex is indeterminate,
in spite of the headdress, earrings, and other ornaments. The
wonderful *modelés* inspired by Leonardo, especially that of a Sibyl not
used for the ceiling of the Sistina, stress the androgynous elements.
More than any other drawing this unforgettable head betrays Michelangelo's longing for the perfect human being. In this lies the secret
of both his and Leonardo's erotic nature. If Michelangelo's figures
tend to be masculine, Leonardo's ideal is more feminine, but both
share the nostalgia for the bisexual perfect being; a longing which
could not be gratified on the worldly level. His early sketches of the
Madonna, like the nude of the Bambino in graphite (in the British
Museum) and the design for a mother and child in black chalk at
the Casa Buonarroti, proclaim the tension and transition from male
to female. The Florentine design of a boyish mother and a feminine
boy is strongly reminiscent of Leonardo, of for example, the 'Madonna
with the Flower' at Munich. It is one of the characteristics of Michelangelo's Holy Virgins that they look away from the Child into the
far distance, as though seeing either perfection or the inevitable
sacrifice of that which is created perfect.

The head for the 'Creation of Adam' (in the British Museum) has a
feminine quality, something of the Renaissance *virago;* in spite of a
certain hesitant quality of line, it radiates an indescribable physical and
spiritual beauty. There had been nothing comparable to it in western
art since the Hellenic dream ended. Only Leonardo and Raphael
approached it, and perhaps Giorgione and Titian. Some Neo-
classicists like David, Ingres and the Pre-Raphaelites, and lastly the
Bavarian painter Anselm Feuerbach tried to revive it. But all subsequent drawings lack the pulse of life which beats in the drawings
of the Florentine master.

In the end Michelangelo abjured this ideal of fifth-century Greece
to which all subsequent generations until the decline of the Roman

Empire had paid tribute. The sketches for the 'Last Judgement' prove this. A thorn is perceptible in the smooth flesh, and the massed bodies of the altar fresco and its preliminary drawings are suddenly full of a gruesome irony; the solid bodies acquire an alarming, truly infernal gravity, a repellent athletic strengh which turns rebelliously against the heavens. The sketches for the 'Last Judgement' were rapidly drawn, obscure and painful explosions of ideas. The figures are nebulous, like clusters of stars. The astonishing graphite and chalk drawings of martyrs and the damned (in the British Museum) include a profusion of moving figures thrown at random on to the paper, not a few of which were transposed on to the fresco wall. Nothing is left of the former clear, classical beauty. The naked writhe and rear, shaken by rage and terror, and here almost more than in the actual frescoes of the Sistine Chapel it seems as though all are cursed and damned.

Nevertheless they are the artist's last revel in the muscular play of powerful bodies; a late flaring-up of the pride and splendour of the Renaissance. The theme, with its wealth of motives, which nourished generations of artists from Rubens to Delacroix and Picasso, is squandered because it dawned on Michelangelo that henceforth he would dispense with such means of expression.

Under the influence of Vittoria Colonna, whose 'divine spirit cloaked him in love', as Condivi says, Michelangelo became a true Christian and could no longer reconcile his Catholic faith with paganism. Now he began to offer his prodigious memory of form and his pleasure in creating it to God, to whom he owed every gift. It would be very short-sighted to assume that this step led to the deterioration of his art or the stifling of his genius. But from now on his art reflected his irrevocable change of heart, to which his grief over Vittoria's death put the seal of finality. Condivi writes: 'He loved her so much that I recall hearing him say that he regretted one thing only: that when he went to see her on her deathbed he did not

DESCENT FROM THE CROSS. *c.*1540-2
CASA BUONARROTI, FLORENCE

kiss her on the forehead and the face but only her hand. He was beside himself over her death!'

In the drawings he made for Vittoria, the change of heart was complete. The 'Last Judgement', and his own day of reckoning, lay behind him. From now on he treated only religious themes expressed in Christian terms, first in the frescoes of Saint Peter and Saint Paul, and later in painted or carved groups of Christ and the Holy Virgin. During the last seventeen years of his life, he was chiefly an architect; the first architect for Christendom. He returned to the theme of the Pietà to which we owe the greatest sculpture of his youth. In the black chalk drawing of Mary the Mother of mankind at the foot of the Cross, holding her dead son supported by angels, the victory of a Christian concept of redemption finds subtle expression; it is the victory of the Son of Man through the faith and intercession of his mother. (A copy from the lost original is at the Isabella Stuart Gardner Museum, Boston.) At the same time this divine mother embodies Vittoria and her victory over Michelangelo's soul, dead to this world, freed to perform its last and greatest deeds. In this perpendicular composition the new Baroque and yet Gothic vertical triumphed over the hedonist horizontal of the Renaissance. This is one of his most finished drawings. The dissolution of corpo-reality in pure linear drawing beginning to appear as through a mist of tears is imminent but not as yet complete.

THE PIETAS

As we have seen, Michelangelo was a solitary and taciturn man. He did not easily admit others into his intimacy and could be harsh and rude, impatient to the point of intolerance, so that others, alarmed by his titanic vision, feared the daemonic forces inherent in him. All the same, one must not form a one-sided assessment of him as a person. Deep within him lay tenderness and humility. In spite of his rages he was generous with his dependents, his pupils, and his noble but coarse-mannered relatives, especially with his grasping nephew Leonardo. His own manners, especially in his old age, were those of an accomplished nobleman, observing an almost Spanish etiquette, who by the quality of his conversation attracted a selective and fastidious company. Many sources testify to this, in particular the four dialogues on painting by the Portuguese Francisco d'Ollanda. In his Roman memoirs *De la Pintura Antiga* published in Lisbon in 1548, Michelangelo is described as the main conversationalist of Vittoria Colonna's circle. Even if these dialogues are not faithful reproductions of what was said by Michelangelo, Vittoria and the others are somewhat stilted and verbose by comparison. D'Ollanda, who was himself sometimes present, has caught something of the atmosphere of these gatherings, and Michelangelo's personality and charm of manner come through very distinctly. We need quote only one sentence of Michelangelo's to convey his conception of the artist: 'In order to reproduce an even partial likeness of Our Lord it is not enough to be a great painter; one must also lead an exemplary life and be as saintly as possible, so that the understanding may be directed by the Holy Ghost.'

This was Michelangelo, and this was how he thought; an example to all true artists, not only by his work but by his whole demeanour. His contemporaries called him *'il terribile'*, and this epithet expressed their respect and fear of the incomprehensible element in his nature, with a dash of malice added for good measure. This quality of strangeness found expression in the 'Deposition from the Cross', placed since 1722 inside the dark nave of Santa Maria del Fiore of Florence, and in a Pietà, moved in 1952 from the Roman Palazzo Rondanini opposite the house where Goethe lived to the Castello of Milan.

Michelangelo could at times be violent, aggressive, even vindictive; he was feared by his adversaries. But in his old age he became mild and gentle, of a touching kindness to those who depended on him. This kindness is expressed in the face of Nicodemus of the Florentine 'Deposition'. For many of Michelangelo's admirers this wonderful head is a self-portrait of the octogenarian. But in ultimate analysis every work by the unique genius portrays a different aspect of his great soul.

In recent times it has often been said that these last sculptures and particularly the 'Pietà Rondanini' whose technique reminds us of

PIETA. *c.* 1548-55
CATHEDRAL, FLORENCE

woodcarvings, were influenced by Rhenish or Flemish masters, perhaps by the Master of Flémalle. Although, as we have seen, with Michelangelo few influences were ever more than superficial, it is clear that the latent Gothic artist in him at last pierced the brilliant surface of Renaissance art, and the cognizance of faith triumphed over mere intellectual knowledge.

Michelangelo, who wished his mortal remains to be buried in Santa Maria Maggiore in Rome, had clearly worked on this memorial group with zest and fury. But fate decreed that the 'Pietà' and his dead body should be brought separately to Florence, and remain separated. The 'Pietà' became the heart of the Duomo, placed in the left-hand choir chapel, while Michelangelo was buried in Santa Croce, together with the remains of other great Italians, in accordance with his last wishes.

Michelangelo knew the healing power of hard work; presumably he embarked on this group of rhomboid shape recalling a bishop's mitre or the dome of Saint Peter's, in order to retain his sanity after Vittoria's death. On arriving in Rome towards the middle of the 16th century, Blaise de Vignère saw the master at work on it. Although he seemed feeble with age, he was hacking huge slices off the marble block with an astonishing precision and without taking a fraction of an inch too much or too little, doing the work of three stone-masons at once. Later, Michelangelo seems to have been dissatisfied with what he had done and smashed it. Commissioned by Francesco Badini a minor sculptor, Tiberio Calcagni, dared to repair and finish the great work, but died just in time to save it from ruin. This is evident from the feminine torso of Christ and the stiff figure of the Magdalene with a glossy finish, to the left.

There are those who believe that Michelangelo gave up this group and smashed it because the left leg of Jesus was not visible, which was an offence against the Renaissance convention. But it is clear that it was fury over his failure with the left arm, the central axis of the composition, which made him abjure what he had done. Be that as it may; we admire this arm and do not miss the left leg because of the intrinsic 'rightness' and inevitablity of the group, and we never cease to be fascinated by the Gothic proportions of the armature. In a work of this calibre the much abused term 'abstract' immediately suggests itself, and yet precisely in this case it would be quite out of place. One ought, on the contrary, to point out that his development drove Michelangelo to a supreme degree of concrete realism. To the very end, the artist strove for form, because he knew the spiritual reality behind it, which is as far removed from abstraction as heaven is from hell. It is useless to look for anything like such feeling for form in Graeco-Roman, or even in Etruscan art. The nearest thing to it is found in the neo-Etruscan Donatello, on one of whose bronze reliefs (at the Victoria and Albert Museum, London) we can see the Christ with an arm twisted and a head bent like that of the 'Pietà' in the Duomo.

The contours of the Florentine 'Pietà' are determined not only by the Romanesque and Gothic arches; as previously stated, it fits into the shape of Saint Peter's dome. To the patient and attentive beholder it will begin to seem as though the group were in the process of growing, perpetually seeking to fill the lofty space with divine sorrow as with the peal of a great bell. The sculpture's august fugue of four voices, from being at first flat and two-dimensional, increases in depth, gaining fresh dimensions, and embraces all the great concepts of Christianity: charity, sacrifice, victory over death, all-embracing humanity, rebirth, salvation, to name only these. It is a truly miraculous image, and the dead Son of Man is alive. His body, upheld by Nicodemus and the two Marys, infuses the whole group with brightness. He has given himself to them, and they have become as one with him. His body forms a circle with the two women and a vertical with Nicodemus and, lo and behold, the composition reveals itself as an interlocked pattern of mystical letters. Some people have read into the rhythm of the limbs the monogram of Jesus Christ combined with A, I and O—that is to say, beginning, middle and end, or Alpha and Omega, with Jesus in the centre.

In what is thought to be Michelangelo's last drawing of the Mother and Son she stands there as the hub of the universe, having found total fulfilment in the child fathered by the spirit. This delicate, transparent drawing of the mother embracing her child (in the British Museum, black chalk) is, as it were, a prologue to the 'Pietà Rondanini'

PALESTRINA PIETA. *c.* 1556
ACCADEMIA, FLORENCE

into which Michelangelo put his ultimate and most tender understanding, after the 'Deposition from the Cross' with the four figures had
failed to satisfy him.

In the end, Michelangelo smashed the 'Pietà Rondanini' which was
really begun before the Florentine 'Pietà', only in order to begin anew
shortly before his death and extract from the remaining fragment
quite a different meaning. He clearly had recurring bouts of fear of
the daemonic forces in his breast which gave him command over
vast creative powers, and, so to speak, enabled him to vie with the
Demiurge. What temerity that called for! And yet this primitive
fear of the powers unleashed by himself was his worst enemy.
Nevertheless his last works suggest that in the end he mastered his
fear. The architectural feats of his later years indicate this, and
most of all it is visible in the apparently spent figures of the 'Pietà
Rondanini'. Theirs is not resignation in the sense of an extinction
of thought, feeling and will in complete despair. It is, rather, a
total renunciation of all that was externally acquired; a complete
detachment achieved by the artist immediately before passing through
the doors of death. It is recorded that six days before his death, the
eighty-eight-year-old master worked on this last symbol of humility
and sacrifice, of poverty in the spirit, declaring himself in the re-worked
upper portion a renegade towards his former self, as Tolstoy did four
hundred years after him. Indeed, almost all the greatest men have
consumed themselves by being the destroyers of their earlier selves
and their works. Their last years are generally marked by open or
unspoken negation of their past with all its achievements. The
Lord hides the mortal body of Moses in Sinai. Under the guise of
Prospero, Shakespeare flings the book containing wisdom into the
ocean. Dante shrouds himself in silence. Many, too weak to bear
the strain, fall a prey to madness. Schiller, Mozart, Beethoven and
Pascal atone in illness. With Michelangelo the gradual renunciation
and abnegation began early, which accounts for the fact that so much
of what he did remained fragmentary. Some critics have attributed
this to a number of external reasons, but in fact it was inherent in his
character and destiny.

The real reasons for his detachment were the deep scars left by

RONDANINI PIETA.   1555-64
CASTELLO SFORZESCO, MILAN

the early loss of his mother, his youth in strange workshops among brutal and arrogant apprentices, the incident with Torrigiani, and the loss of Vittoria Colonna. But the crux of the matter lay elsewhere —in his astonishingly clear-cut individuality which, in spite of making him extremely sensitive to atmosphere and circumstances, was essentially independent. His will was far too strong to be swayed by marginalia. One may say that instead of being influenced by the spirit of this age, he determined it—or, with unerring certainty, extracted from it what he needed. This would explain his periodical times of doubt and confusion and his repeated retreats. He was, so to speak, born to be a saint, but had to reach sainthood by the way of art. It is therefore erroneous to claim Michelangelo either for the Renaissance, for Mannerism or for the Baroque. He put the stamp of his own personality on the period into which he was born.

In the 'Pietà Rondanini' one can clearly distinguish between his attitude before and after his 'rebirth' (which still left him mortal!); before and after acquiring consciousness of the divine spark in his own being. One might be tempted to say that in him the distinction between physical body and spiritual body is made manifest, but with the reservation that while the former is complete and fully developed, the latter had hardly begun to form when he came face to face with death. The master left this work neither to the Pope nor to a great noble, nor to any person of his circle. He bequeathed it to the simplest man he could find, his servant Antonio del Francese, perhaps one of the meek and humble of whom it is said that they shall inherit the earth. The legacy was virtually a gift to God, as was Brückner's last symphony, dedicated to the Maker.

Originally, the Christ of the 'Pietà Rondanini' faced to the left, the head falling on to the right shoulder of his athletic body; but this was the part that Michelangelo broke. Of it, only the lower arm and a portion of the upper arm are left. In the final version the head rests squarely on the powerful torso of the Saviour. The mother, whose head rises above his own, supports him; at the same time she seems borne upward by the Christ. Mother and Son detach themselves from the nether region and ascend to eternity like a pair of lovers; just so did Paolo and Francesca escape from the

TOMB OF MICHELANGELO
SANTA CROCE, FLORENCE

gates of hell—and this is no unseemly comparison. The epitome of man's salvation is expressed here; it is reunion of the sundered elements, banished from heaven by a fall from grace. The blending of the two heads may be approximate and incomplete; it none the less remains the master's last word; it is a silent word, and for us it has become synonymous with silence.

Michelangelo Buonarroti died on 18th February 1564 to, as Vasari puts it, 'depart for a better life'.

TEXT REFERENCES

1. The *Zohar* was the title of a collection of heterogeneous writings of uncertain origin and mystical content. The author may have been Moise ben Chtomb of Leon, but probably he merely translated it from a much older script, mostly in an Aramaic dialect. The brightness refers to divine Mind, or illumination, and the *Zohar* contains psychological teaching and cosmological speculation, a doctrine of emanation encyphered in a theory of numbers.
'And I looked, and behold, a whirlwind came out of the north, a great cloud, and a fire unfolding itself, and a brightness was about it, and out of the midst thereof as the colour of amber, out of the midst of the fire.' (Ezekiel 1,4) 'Then I beheld, and lo a likeness as the appearance of fire; and from the appearance of his loins even downward, fire; and from his loins even upward, as the appearance of brightness, as the colour of amber.' (Ezekiel 8,3). 'And they that be wise (or teachers) shall shine as the brightness of the firmament; and they that turn many to righteousness as the stars forever and ever'. (Daniel 12,3). *Transl.*

2. Dante identifies them with Contessa Matilda di Canossa, the alleged ancestor of Michelangelo. Rachel and Leah, the wives of Jacob, figure in *Purgatorio* as symbols of the passive and active life. *Transl.*

3. This sonnet is never satisfactory in translation. The image is of steam absorbed by heat but clouding the vision, and of a process of dissolution. 'Onde' means literally 'therefore' and refers to the cold heart. The half line 'che 'l foco ammerza' is an interpolation signifying 'only the love of God can melt the hardness of self love'. *Transl.*

4. This sonnet, kept in the *Codice Vaticano*, was sent by Michelangelo to Vasari with an accompanying note. (The image of Christ opening his arms wide on the Cross is lost in translation.) *Transl.*

5. *Inferno* 106-108. Translation: H.F. Carey, 1805.

LIST OF ILLUSTRATIONS

INDEX OF NAMES